On a Mission

On a Mission

Mamadou's Wedding and My Naming Ceremony

A Memoir

Jane Banks McIntosh

iUniverse, Inc.
New York Lincoln Shanghai

On a Mission
Mamadou's Wedding and My Naming Ceremony

iUniverse books may be ordered through booksellers or by contacting:

iUniverse
2021 Pine Lake Road, Suite 100
Lincoln, NE 68512
www.iuniverse.com
1-800-Authors (1-800-288-4677)

ISBN: 978-0-595-42257-9 (pbk)
ISBN: 978-0-595-86594-9 (ebk)

Printed in the United States of America

CONTENTS

Mamadou's Wedding

My Naming Ceremony

Mamadou's Wedding

Following my Pilgrimage to Senegal and The Gambia, the McIntosh family in California and Ohio kept in close touch by phone and mail back and forth with Mamadou Niang's family and Madame Gueye's family in Dakar. Since our familial bonding with Mamadou during our Pilgrimage, he had adopted me as his other mother, affectionately addressing me and referring to me as "Mum Jane" and calling Birdie "Sister Birdie," even to this day.

Mamadou was a tall, handsome African man in his early thirties. He was slender. He flashed a warm smile; his eyes sparkled when he fixed them on yours when he spoke. He was fluent in English, French, and of course his ethnic language, Wolof. His delivery was deliberate and distinct. I was instantly impressed that he stood erect, took long strides when he walked, and carried himself regally.

One cold, dreary, rainy, winter day in early November, I was down in my study, writing. Mamadou phoned from Dakar. Of course, getting a call from him was always a surprise and a delight, but this time it was unusually surprising because it hadn't been that long since we'd talked. I heard a euphoric excitement in his voice as, all in one breath, he exclaimed, "Mum Jane, I'm getting married on December 24, and I want you and Sister Birdie to come to my wedding here in Dakar."

Spontaneously and without thinking through any of the requirements or details, I congratulated him and accepted his invitation.

"I am going to call Sister Birdie right now so both of you can begin making your plans," he added.

There was something in his voice besides ecstasy. It denoted brevity. So I didn't prolong our conversation. We said goodbye.

My husband, Gaines, and I were both retired. After forty-three years of marriage, we'd been blessed to be able to luxuriate in our slow-paced, low-key lifestyle at home in Hayward, California. Our son, Arthur Ross, his wife, Birdie, and our grandchildren and great-grandchildren lived and worked in and around the vicinity of Cincinnati, Ohio.

Preoccupied in my own cosmic space, I left my study, and as I walked up the stairs to the TV room to tell Gaines, I thought aloud, "What will Gaines say? Did I just commit myself to return to Dakar after just seventeen months? Has God answered my prayer to spare me to be able to revisit my Motherland? Will Birdie be able to get time off from work to make the trip at this time of year?"

While sharing the news from Mamadou with Gaines, the phone rang again. I answered and heard Birdie's voice shouting, "Mum Jane, I just finished talking with Mamadou." This was unlike Birdie who had such a soft, well-modulated voice. She was almost shrieking. Then, I suddenly realized that we were both talking at the same time. Mostly, we were asking each other over and over again, "What did you say? What did you tell him? What did you say? What did you tell him?"

I stopped talking and listened carefully to her. I could visualize the expression on her face as she slowly and deliberately asked, "Mum Jane, what did *you* tell him?"

"Without even giving it a second thought, I told him that I accepted his invitation," I answered.

In return, I asked her, "What did *you* tell him?"

She had calmed down somewhat, and between breaths, she answered, "I told him I'd talk with you about it, and if at all possible, we'd be there. I told him it would be an honor to attend his wedding … especially since it would be held in Dakar."

I told Birdie to begin making our travel plans through the agency that had so competently arranged our Pilgrimage.

"OK, I'll begin immediately. Just think," she said convincingly, "we'll be able to go back to our Motherland again and spend time with Mamadou and his family and Madame Gueye and her family. Maybe we'll even be able to travel to The Gambia and see the girls and Isha."

While she was talking, bits and pieces of past experiences flashed through my mind—experiences we'd shared just seventeen months before. My heart was pounding with excitement. I knew then and there that if life lasted for me, we'd witness Mamadou's marriage in Dakar, Senegal, West Africa.

Senegal was my favorite of the two countries I'd visited on my Pilgrimage. The country was a self-governed republic, having gained independence from France in 1960. French was the official language and was spoken fluently. However, there were some seventeen different tribal languages spoken. In other words, each tribe had its own language. Mamadou's family and Madame Gueye's family belonged to the Wolof tribe. They all spoke their ethnic Wolof language, as well as French. Some Senegalese people spoke a little English. The majority of the population practiced the Muslim religion.

I found the Senegalese people to be very cordial and friendly. They demonstrated a deep concern about the people of other countries, as well themselves. Their eyes lit up whenever I came among them. Wherever I went, I was greeted with warm smiles, but beneath the surface, I sensed an expression of curiosity or inspiring awe.

A week or so later, Mamadou called me again. His tone of voice was prideful and emphatic, but with deliberate excitement, he announced, "Mum Jane, I'm so happy to learn through Madame Gueye that you and Sister Birdie have begun making plans to come to Dakar for my wedding. She informs me that you have requested reservations at the Hotel Sofitel Teranga in Dakar. As a result, Madame Gueye has asked me to call you to invite you and Sister Birdie to be her houseguests. We do not want you to stay in a hotel while you are here with us in your Motherland. You are family, and we want you to stay with your family."

Needless to say, I accepted, saying, "Please extend our thanks and deep appreciation to Madame Gueye. Tell her that we are honored to accept her invitation to be her houseguests."

I couldn't dial the numbers fast enough to call Birdie to share the news with her.

She answered the phone, and I told her about our special invitation. She sounded ecstatic as she exclaimed, "Oh, Mum Jane, that's just wonderful! That's just wonderful! Here's another opportunity for us to share an extraordinary experience in our Motherland."

We talked for a while longer, and like two teenage girls, promised to keep each other informed of all developments.

Later on, we learned that during that time, Madame Gueye was working for Africa Connection Tours which was the travel agency through which we were requesting our accommodations. One of her duties was making hotel reservations for visitors to Dakar. When she received the request from our travel agent to reserve a room for us at the Hotel Sofitel Teranga where we stayed on our Pilgrimage, she immediately informed Mamadou that our request had come through. It was at that time that she told Mamadou to call and extend her invitation to us to be her houseguests when we came to Dakar to attend his wedding on December 24.

Madame Gueye was a middle-aged, married Senegalese woman. She and her husband had four children who were now young adults. The family lived in a beautiful, custom-built home. Her husband was a retired building contractor who designed and built their home in what appeared to me to be an affluent neighborhood on the outskirts of Dakar. Her eyes lit up when she smiled, baring her pearly white teeth. She had a stylish flair as she walked. One night on our Pilgrimage at dinner in their home, she wore a red and black print, ankle-length dress that hung loosely over her firm, rounded torso. When I complimented her garment, she was quick to tell me that she was a seamstress and that she designed and made most of the garments in her wardrobe.

Neither Arthur Ross nor his father, Gaines, chose to sacrifice their time or spend the money to go to Mamadou's wedding. Therefore, when Gaines and I reminded each other that never during our married years had we been apart during the Christmas season, we decided to fly to Cincinnati together. There, I would join Birdie for our trip to Dakar, and Gaines could spend Christmas with Arthur Ross and the rest of the family living in that area.

All during the preparation for our departure, I was driven by the excitement of being with Mamadou when he got married. At the same time, my mind was flooded with recollections of some of the many faces—some young, some old. I kept seeing Senegal's emblem, the baobab tree with its huge, twisted trunk. They call it the "tree of life," because all parts of the tree provide some substance for life. I recalled that during a lecture, I was told that the tree can live to be hundreds of years old and that the trunk of the largest baobab tree is so gigantic that as many as fifteen men with outstretched arms cannot encircle it.

But tucked away in my mind was the deep impact of my heart-wrenching experience at Le Maison des Esclaves on Gorée Island, which was built for the sole purpose of "storing" Africans awaiting shipment across the Atlantic Ocean to be sold in the Western world.

Our plans moved forward without incident, and the synchronization was perfect. When Gaines and I landed in Cincinnati, Art and Birdie met our arriving flight. We said our good-byes. Gaines and Art left for home on Egan Hills Drive in Cincinnati. Birdie and I positioned ourselves for departure from Cincinnati to Newark, New Jersey, where our travel agent had made reservations for us to spend the night in order to catch our flight to Dakar from JFK the next day.

On Our Way

That flight to Newark was uneventful—just anticipatory and pensive. We asked each other lots of questions, but neither of us had any answers. The one answer we did have and agreed upon was that we were operating completely on blind faith and anticipation as to what we'd experience, and even encounter. But nothing else really mattered, because we were on our way back to our Motherland for Mamadou's wedding.

As we landed in Newark, Birdie declared in no uncertain terms, "Jane, we're going on a 'mission'!"

I couldn't help hearing what she said, but somehow, it didn't quite register or click in at the moment.

We took a shuttle from the airport to the hotel and checked in.

Before leaving the counter, in her travel-experienced voice, Birdie asked the reservations clerk, "Do you have a morning shuttle to the airport?"

"Oh yes," he replied. As he pointed to his left he said, "And the departure time is posted on the easel."

We purchased our shuttle tickets and followed the bellman as he took our luggage to our room. Quickly, we got settled in. We took the elevator down to the restaurant on the first floor, had dinner, and promptly went back up to our room to get a good night's sleep so we could get up early enough to have a leisurely breakfast and then take the shuttle from the hotel to JFK to catch our flight.

Off to Dakar

So there we were, Birdie and me, in Newark, New Jersey, on our way to JFK International Airport to catch our flight to Dakar, Senegal, West Africa. And, as planned, we got up early enough to have that leisurely breakfast in the hotel restaurant.

We headed for the hotel lobby with all of our baggage and checked the shuttle departure time posted on the easel near the reservations counter. There was open seating in the restaurant, so we seated ourselves at a small table and placed our orders. We ate leisurely as we asked each other some more of the same perplexing questions we had asked each other time and time again.

After breakfast, we wandered around in the gift shop and then meandered back to the lobby to check the shuttle departure time again.

Alas! The easel was gone. There was no easel.

Walking and talking, Birdie asked frantically, "Where's the easel?"

Bewildered, I said to Birdie "They moved it."

As I looked at my watch, I followed Birdie. She confidently stepped up to the counter and interrupted the agent who was serving another guest. All in one breath, she asked the agent, "Where's the easel? What time does the shuttle leave for JFK?"

In a regretful tone of voice, the agent took a fleeting glance at the international time clock on the wall behind him. Looking back at us, he said, "Oh, I'm sorry, but that shuttle's gone. It left ten minutes ago."

As if our world had fallen apart, we looked at each other and turned away from the counter.

I said to Birdie, "I can't believe that after having mastered all of the preparatory details, here we are with our tickets, passports, visas, International Certificates of Vaccination as approved by the World Health Organization, and airport shuttle tickets. But we missed our shuttle from here to JFK."

We turned back to the desk attendant. Birdie asked, "What other means of transportation can we get to take us to JFK to catch our international flight?"

The attendant was quick to respond, "The only other means of transportation is by taxicab. And there's a cabstand right out front, shortly to your left. You can get one right away, because there are cabs parked there 24/7."

We thanked him profusely and left the lobby. With all that baggage, we hurried to the cabstand.

Birdie told the first driver she saw, "We need to get to JFK airport as soon as possible. We are booked on an international flight."

I don't think the driver spoke or understood much English, but he understood her well enough to say, "No problem. No problem," as he pointed to his taxi.

We watched him as he put our luggage in the trunk. We hopped in the back seat, and the driver took off.

It was morning rush hour, and the outbound highway traffic was horrendous, as was the inbound and inner-city traffic. The ride was long and noisy. As if the driver could do anything but keep driving, Birdie kept reminding him of our flight departure time.

Assuredly in his broken English, he again said, "No problem. No problem."

Even so, I was apprehensive because it seemed to me that the taxi ride was interminable.

In spite of our faux pas, we arrived at JFK in plenty of time. We went through customs and immigration, checked our luggage, and got our boarding passes. With all that behind us, we were able to get seats side by side and relax in the boarding area. At last, we were unencumbered. We looked at each other, giggled, and breathed a deep sigh of relief.

There were so many people milling around in the boarding area, I asked Birdie, "Do you think all of these people are going on the same flight with us?"

She replied confidently, "No. Look on the board. There's a flight leaving just before ours, but it's also boarding through the same gate as our flight."

I physically and mentally relaxed. Momentarily, I felt arrogant since we had plenty of time before flight time. For a few minutes, we sat there just people-watching.

Suddenly, as if she had forgotten something, Birdie stood up and said, "Mum Jane, I'm going to the duty-free shop. You stay here and watch our bags."

"OK, and then when you come back, I'll go while you watch the bags," I answered, gathering our possessions closer to my feet so I could keep a close eye on everything. There I sat, watching people with a worthless airport shuttle ticket I'd purchased the night before. Inwardly, I begrudged having had to share that enormous taxicab fare from Newark, New Jersey to JFK.

Birdie came back. When she sat down, I didn't see any packages. I asked her, "You didn't buy anything?"

"Yes, I made a purchase, but the clerk told me I could pick it up after I'm cleared through the boarding gate," she answered.

So since she was back, I went to the duty-free shop. On the way, a myriad of sentimental thoughts kept popping up in my mind—sentimental thoughts like, *I'm going back to Africa, my Motherland. There, I'll get to see some of my African brothers and sisters again. I'll get to see Mamadou, my* sama dome *(Wolof for "other son") again. And we'll be privileged to witness his marriage.* So many thoughts flooded my mind that I walked right past the entrance to the shop. I had to retrace my steps.

While browsing, I could hear a flight being called for boarding. I hurriedly made my selections. The cashier told me I could retrieve my purchases after clearing the boarding gate, just as Birdie said the cashier had told her.

I walked back to my seat and when I got there, Birdie told me, "That other flight was called for passengers to board."

"Yes, I heard the call, and that's why I hurried back. Our flight will be next," I muttered with bated breath.

Only moments later, our flight was called. I was amused as we both simultaneously sprung up from our seats as if we'd been shot from a cannon, picked up our carry-on luggage and unhurriedly headed for the boarding gate.

With a broad smile, Birdie turned to me and said, "Jane! We're getting ready to board our plane. We're going on a mission!"

My breaths were short, and my heart was pounding. I think I was hyperventilating, but I managed to answer, "Yes! We're on our way," as we took our places in line to board Air Afrique for Dakar.

Although the excitement of it all surged in my bosom, I was gripped by a prayerful mood. At that moment, again I thanked God for answering my prayer. He had blessed me to be able to return to my Motherland. I, Mamadou's other mother (*sama yaye* in Wolof), was on my way to board the plane for the flight to witness the marriage of my other son, *sama dome*.

We inched along in line to where the airline attendant was stationed. She examined our documents and directed us to proceed to the counter to pick up our duty-free packages.

It was fascinating to me that most of the passengers were loaded down with carry-on luggage, huge stuffed animals, large sealed boxes, great big holiday gift-wrapped packages, and oversized plastic shopping bags bulging with stuff.

So that no one would hear me, I took a step closer and asked Birdie, "Why are these people allowed to have so many carry-ons?"

"I was wondering that myself but didn't want to mention it," she said.

I kept my voice as low as possible and said, "I guess all that stuff is for family and friends in Senegal. But I packed Isha's doll and the bag of school supplies in one of my luggage pieces, and all of that baggage is checked."

"The bag of cosmetics is checked in my luggage for the girls in The Gambia," she assured me.

Finally, we arrived at the gate. As soon as we got there, we checked again to verify our flight number, departure time, and destination posted on the board behind the Air Afrique counter. Comfortable in the fact that unlike the first time, we'd been mindful to reserve our seats. Side by side we sat patiently waiting as we watched most of the other passengers getting seat assignments just before boarding.

After nearly everyone else had boarded, Birdie and I confidently strolled into the cabin, taking in all of the sights and sounds.

We could hear conversations and laughter even before we got into the cabin of the plane, but as we entered, we were warmly welcomed aboard by two attendants—one male and one female. Other attendants were also on board. From their accents, I think they were Africans.

As we walked down the aisle checking for our seat numbers, Birdie said, "Jane, this plane is full."

Boastfully, I said, "But we don't have to worry, because we reserved our seats side by side on this flight—not like the first time."

"You got that right," she replied.

"Yes, how well I remember that kind young African man who traded seats with you so we could sit together," I reminded Birdie as we flopped down.

Again Birdie excitedly exclaimed, "Mum Jane! We're going on a mission. We're going on a mission."

What she'd just said registered with me for the first time. I remembered that she had said that before. In fact, she'd said it several times before. This time, I thought about it, and I agreed with her. "You know, I hadn't thought of it in that light until just now, but it's true, Birdie. We are going on a mission," I acknowledged.

As we situated our carry-ons, the flight attendants busied themselves with their tasks of making us comfortable and offering pillows. We each took a pillow and settled in for our flight across the Atlantic Ocean.

Birdie reiterated, "Jane! We're going back to Africa. We're going to witness Mamadou's marriage."

My mind flipped into a whirlwind. As I nestled back into my seat, everything about the plane seemed so familiar. In fact, it didn't seem as though it had been only about a year and a half since I had been aboard that other Air Afrique flight to Dakar.

As I looked around, just as before, the passengers were a mix of races, colors, sizes, and nationalities. I could identify most of the passengers as African, dozens as African American, some as African European, some as Asian, and some as Asian Americans. Others, I couldn't identify, because I couldn't distinguish their ethnicity. And there was a mix of many languages spoken in conversation back and forth with one another and across the aisles.

Here we were again, Birdie and I aboard the same flight and on the same plane that had taken us to and brought us back from our Pilgrimage to our Motherland. I kept thinking about my prayer as I'd left Senegal on my way back to America and every single day since my return home to Hayward. Silently, I again thanked God for answering my prayer that He would bless me to be able to return to my Motherland.

My heart swelled with pride as we were welcomed aboard by a low-pitched, authoritative male voice in clear English, who said, "This is your captain speaking. Welcome aboard this Air Afrique Flight from JFK International Airport to Léopold Senghor International Airport in Dakar, Senegal. It is my wish and the wishes of the entire crew that you have a pleasant flight, because we intend to do everything possible to ensure just that. So settle back and enjoy the flight."

The attendants had gotten everybody settled into their seats and checked the overhead bins as they strolled the aisles. At that moment, we were moving.

The captain's words were comforting. It felt good to sit back, relax, and think about our trip. I was on my way back to my Motherland. Only this time, we were, as Birdie had so aptly named it, on a "mission." More importantly, it was a mission of singular significance. We were on our way back home as special invited guests to attend the traditional Islamic African wedding of Mamadou, my *sama dome,* and Sister Birdie's African brother who had adopted us when we bonded into our African family on our Pilgrimage the previous year.

As we lifted off, we pinpointed our location and began to chart our course on the giant-sized monitor. Every few minutes, the flight information was updated in French and English. Of course, the airplane icon was just barely moving, so I could see that we hadn't really left New York yet.

When we reached cruising altitude, the attendants began gingerly moving about in the utility area. It wasn't long before I got a whiff of aromas from food. There was no doubt in my mind that already the crew was preparing a meal to serve us. "Something sure smells good," I shared with Birdie.

She agreed and reminded me, "You know, we haven't eaten since early this morning in that hotel restaurant."

"I guess I've been so engrossed in the happenings of our day's experiences, I didn't even think about food," I admitted.

By that time, we could pinpoint our location. I took out my journal and noted that we were already out over the Atlantic Ocean, flying at 660 miles an hour at a ground speed of 582 miles an hour. We had a tailwind of 65 miles an hour, and we were at an altitude of thirty-seven thousand feet. The temperature was fifty degrees below zero outside. Ah! But it was warm and cozy inside.

Just then the attendants began taking orders for beverages.

We exchanged comments about the camaraderie throughout the cabin. There was so much jovial conversation and exuberance among the passengers that I reminded Birdie that it was just four days before Christmas.

No sooner than the beverage glasses had been collected, to my delight, our meal was served. The entrée was filet mignon, baked potato, a crisp salad of lettuce and cherry tomatoes, French bread; there was ice cream for dessert, and a complimentary bottle of wine.

The steak was so tender I could cut it with my fork; the potato was hot, soft, and mushy, just the way I like a baked potato.

As I lavishly spread the butter on my potato, Birdie teasingly said, "Jane, relish that potato, because after we get to Dakar, it'll be rice every day." We both giggled.

"You're right. I probably won't have any more potatoes until I get back home, because we'll be having rice every day. And then I won't want any more rice for the rest of my life."

We both laughed a little louder as we took another sip of dinner wine.

My mouth watered as I lavishly spread my French bread with butter. In anticipation of my first bite, I almost drooled.

"Birdie, what do you think we should expect to happen at this traditional African Islamic wedding?"

"Mum Jane, I don't know. I just don't know," she acknowledged.

"But honestly, the one thing I do know is that Mamadou told me the wedding would last all day long. Now that really puzzles me," I warned.

It was as if she'd been pondering the same thing when she asked me, "Why does a wedding have to last all day long?"

"I can't imagine why," I admitted, shaking my head.

"I can't, either, but we'll soon find out," she answered as she took another sip of wine.

"Oh, Birdie, we haven't discussed what we'll give Mamadou and his bride for a wedding gift," I mused, trying to figure out what she'd say.

"I've been thinking about that, too, but I don't have a clue," she admitted. (We would get our clue later as the wedding day drew closer.)

"Do you think that as African Americans, we'll fit in?" she asked.

"I don't think Mamadou would've told us he wanted us to be there with him if he thought we as African-Americans wouldn't fit in," I said, defending him and sharing my hope and wish with her.

Almost before I'd finished my hope and wish, she volunteered, "And Madame Gueye surely wouldn't have invited us to be her houseguests during our stay if she didn't think we'd fit in."

Confidently, I agreed with her. "You're right, because they treat us like we're a part of their African family. In fact, Mamadou and Madame Gueye have told me that we are a part of their family. It's just that, unfortunately, we haven't known each other for all of our lives."

"Did Mamadou tell you on the phone that the wedding would be held at his home and how many people he expected to attend?" I asked Birdie.

She turned to me with a puzzled look and said, "Yes. He said there would be about three hundred people there. Now how in the world is he going to fit three hundred people into his house?"

Since it had been our unexpected pleasure to have Mamadou take us to his home when we were there on our Pilgrimage, both of us candidly shared our concerns as to how he planned to accommodate that many people. Of course, our only parallel was American weddings and receptions which we African Americans had patterned after in the blanching process of our assimilation into a European American ethos and lifestyle.

"This is going to be very interesting," she said in a tone of finality. And since neither one of us could come up with a conclusion, we mutually abandoned the subject.

Remembering that in recent telephone conversations, Mamadou told me that he had ordered our gowns to be tailor-made from measurements I faxed to him at his request some weeks before, I opened up my concern about the color, style, fabric, and fit of our gowns.

I asked Birdie, "I wonder what our gowns are going to be like."

Birdie excitedly admitted, "I can't wait to see what guests' African wedding gowns look like. I wonder if they'll fit us."

I confessed, "I wonder that, too. In fact, I didn't want to sound uncertain or doubtful, so I haven't said anything to you about the gowns since I sent Mamadou our measurements for his tailor. So let's just wait and see." I was hoping I could dismiss the idea from my mind, but truthfully, I was seriously apprehensive.

To lighten the burden of the subject of the gowns and how three hundred people could be accommodated at the wedding and reception, I appeased myself by saying, "But just think how we're being specially honored by Madame Gueye's asking us to be guests in her home while we're in Dakar for this once-in-a-lifetime opportunity to be a part of a traditional Islamic African wedding."

I guess I drifted off to sleep, because when I aroused, my tray was gone. The attendants were walking up and down the aisle, checking for passenger requests. Another followed with warm wet washcloths. Of course, I took one, thanked her and wiped my sleepy face. Oh, I felt so good and refreshed after my catnap. As another attendant came through the cabin collecting the washcloths, I was again amused by the laughter and gaiety among the passengers and wondered how I could have slept through the din.

Shortly afterwards, the attendants came through with sandwiches and beverages.

Birdie said, "It looks like they're going to serve us some more food."

Even though I hadn't worked up an appetite, I had *slept* up one. We both took sandwiches and beverages of choice.

Birdie gasped, "Jane, this is enough food for our evening meal."

My mouth was salivating again. Between chews, Birdie reminded me that if we're offered food while we're in Dakar, we must remember not to refuse, because it's Senegalese custom to accept what is offered to you.

"I'm glad they told us about their custom. It would be considered impolite to refuse whether you're hungry or not," I confessed.

"But we'll probably be hungry again by then," I said, nodding my head in her direction. We both love to eat, and so we laughed at each other as we chomped away on our sandwiches made with tasty tissue-paper-thin sliced meats and cheeses on that familiar-tasting French bread.

Just then I had a flashback from my Pilgrimage and thought in anticipation about some more of those native dishes we'd be savoring again.

I looked up at the monitor and said, "I can't believe we're almost there."

Birdie reminded me, "The flight is just six and a half hours from New York to Dakar."

As soon as she got it out of her mouth, I could feel that we were losing altitude and that our speed had been markedly reduced in preparation for landing. A quick look at the monitor confirmed that we were coming down for landing.

"Oh! I'm so excited, I can hardly contain myself," I said. No longer trying to be unassuming, and to regain my composure, I took several deep breaths.

"In just a half hour or so, we'll be landing in Dakar," Birdie read as she looked at the monitor. I noticed that she had already prematurely begun to gather up her belongings in anticipation of our landing. Repeating her exclamation, she vowed, "Yes, Mum Jane, we're about to embark on our mission." There was a tone of new determination and excitement in her voice.

I looked up, and the attendant was at our aisle. She assured us that there were plenty of sandwiches and beverages, and we were welcome to have as many as we wanted. We weren't demure, but instead, were eager and fervent in replenishing from the repast.

It seemed that just after our attendants collected the remains, and I began to nestle back in my seat, the captain's voice came through loud and clear, "Will the attendants please prepare for landing at Léopold Senghor International Airport in Dakar, Senegal, West Africa."

The captain enunciated our landing site so clearly and profoundly that I recalled some facts from my research. I had learned that this airport was named after a man named Léopold Sédar Senghor, a Senegalese political leader and poet. Senghor was born in what was formerly French West Africa (now Senegal). He was a learned man, educated at the University of Paris. He began teaching in Tours, France, in 1935. During World War II he served in the French army, was captured and held as a prisoner by the Germans from 1940 to 1943. After his release, he taught at the National College of France. During that time, he became politically active and published articles on both politics and literature which won renown for him as Africa's leading intellectual. As far back as the 1940s, he was credited with having consistently worked for Senegalese independence. Senghor subsequently became the first president of the Republic of Senegal in 1960 and was overwhelmingly reelected in 1966 and 1973.

We fastened our seatbelts, sat there quietly, looked at each other, and at the same time, giggled like two school kids.

Again, Birdie said, "Jane, we're about to arrive and go on our mission!"

"Yep, we're almost there," I said.

Just then, we landed. The landing was so smooth that I couldn't feel the impact when the pilot set down the wheels of the plane on the landing strip. I hadn't realized that my ears were stopped up until they miraculously popped open.

Loudly and clearly, the attendant advised, "Please remain seated until the aircraft comes to a complete stop."

In spite of her admonition, I could hear the hustle and bustle of passengers gathering up their belongings. In a few minutes, the pilot turned off the seatbelt sign.

Earnestly, Birdie and I began gathering up our personal effects and stepped out into the aisle. From there, we had to inch our way toward the exit.

Birdie was talking, and I was talking, but neither of us was making any sense. It's clear to me now that our chatter was just anticipatory nonsense. Though it was nonsensical, it didn't seem to make much difference to either of us as we continued inching our way down the aisle.

When we got to the exit, there stood the pilot, co-pilot, and attendants all smiling as they bade us farewell by saying, "Welcome home!"

We thanked them and left the cabin.

Welcome Home

When I saw the portable stairs, I immediately remembered from our landing at Léopold Senghor the first time, and I said to Birdie, "I forgot that we didn't land at the terminal. Instead, we had to walk down some portable stairs to the concourse where we were directed to board motor coaches that took us to the terminal."

"Right. I forgot, too, until just now when I saw the ladder," she replied.

Passengers were loading onto motor coaches that were lined up. The motors were noisy, and the exhaust fumes were stifling, but we boarded the third bus. That was the first one on which there were any seats. We rode a short distance, and before the driver could stop the bus, passengers created a traffic jam as they rushed from the back of the bus to the front door. Birdie and I just sat quietly until the jam cleared. When the motor coach came to a stop at the curb in front of the entrance to the terminal, we picked up our bags and inched our way to the exit.

On the way, again Birdie said, "Mum Jane, we're on a mission. We're in Dakar, Senegal, West Africa, where we'll be reuniting with our African family."

Choked up in my throat I squeaked out, "Yes, Birdie, we're here again. I thank God for answering my prayer."

"It'll be so good to see Mamadou again, and I can't wait to meet his bride-to-be. I wonder what she's like, and if she's right for Mamadou," Birdie mused.

"Well, we'll know soon," I said as we pulled up in front of the terminal. It was a very short ride.

We got off and walked into the terminal. We took our places in line with other passengers headed for the immigration officer's booth. We moved along painstakingly slow with the crowd. As we got closer to his booth, I could see that the immigration officers were busy checking the documents of each passenger. There had been several hundred of us on that flight.

It was hard to believe that I was standing on the same African soil where I had been a year and a half before. For a moment, it was like reliving that experience as I inched along in line.

"Where's Mamadou? Where's Mamadou?" we were both asking each other since he had assured us that he would be at the airport when we arrived.

Slowly moving along with the crowd as we followed the sign to immigration, we made a right turn from the window. I was in front of Birdie, so when I got to the window, I surrendered my documents.

After I handed over my passport to the officer, he looked up at me, smiled, and said, "Welcome home, sister."

Suddenly, I remembered that on my Pilgrimage. From behind the glass in the immigration officer's window, the officer looked directly at me and asked, "You McIntosh?" He spoke very clearly and in plain English, so there was no mistake as to what he had asked me. Nevertheless, I was dumbfounded—so much so that I couldn't speak. I just stood there, staring at him for a few seconds until he asked me the same question again, except louder and more emphatically, "You McIntosh?" Somehow by then I was able to speak and answered, "Yes." Then, almost as if the scenario had been choreographed, a young African man walked up to us, smiled, extended his hand, and introduced himself as the representative from the tour company. He explained that he had been assigned to meet us and assist us with in the entry process.

To this day, I don't know how he singled me out from among the throng of passengers inching their way to his window to get processed for entry into the country.

I wondered for a moment if this was the same immigration officer and if he had remembered me, my document, my picture, or the incident upon my first arrival. Oh no, that couldn't be. So I simply said, "Thank you. Thank you." For the time being, I gave it no more thought, and concluded that after seeing the information on my passport, he was just welcoming me to my Motherland.

There, as close as he could possibly get to us, stood Mamadou! I saw him before he saw us. He had an anxious look on his face, and his head and eyes were scanning the crowd. As soon as I was sure that it was he, I began waving my hand high in the air so he could see it.

When he saw my hand high in the air, he began waving back with his hand held high in the air.

I shouted to Birdie, "There he is! There's Mamadou! There he is!"

There he stood with that broad smile across his face. His facial expression changed from anxiety to a smile of joy. He was surrounded by an entourage. Beside and behind him was a sea of smiling faces—some familiar and some not familiar. There stood Mamadou, his brother, his sister, his niece, Madame Gueye, and several others whom I didn't recognize.

Birdie and I and all of them were approaching each other at the same time. They were all smiling, some waving back and forth and others waving frantically up and down to get our attention.

I was so excited to see them that I was numb, but I just kept moving like a zombie. I looked around, and Birdie was right beside me for what was a climactic reunion with our family in Africa. She was grinning from ear to ear. I guess I was grinning, too.

Overcome by the fact that so many people had come with Mamadou to welcome us back home, we ran to them, and they ran to us, all chattering at the same time. We all hugged and embraced one another. It was truly an emotional homecoming as we got around to hugging everyone as they said, "Welcome home! Welcome home! Welcome back to your Motherland!" It was as if they had rehearsed their English in order to be able to greet us in our language.

And then everyone was saying something all at the same time and in unison. So I asked Mamadou, "What are they saying?"

In his own inimitable way, he said emphatically, "Mum Jane, they are saying, Welcome home! Welcome home! Welcome home! Welcome home!"

All I could say was, *"Jeredef! Jeredef!"* ("Thank you" in Wolof.) So that they'd be able to understand me a little bit, I had practiced up on a few Wolof phrases just before leaving on our "mission." Of course, Mamadou, his brother, his niece, and Madame Gueye all spoke English, so they could figure out the other nervous chatter from us and translate it to the ones who didn't understand English.

Arm in arm, and again like we were two little girls, Mamadou slowly led Birdie and me to the baggage carousel. He asked us for our claim checks.

We stood there for a moment just looking at each other and then hugging each other again.

He asked us, "How was your flight?"

"Just wonderful," we assured him.

"This landing was just as smooth as the previous landing. I didn't really feel it when the pilot set down on the runway," I said to him.

He said, "Really?" (That was a response he frequently used.)

I said, "Yes, really."

Smiling and giving us another hug, he said, "That's good! That's good!"

There was only a short wait before our luggage came around on the carousel. As we stood there, I noticed that Mamadou looked very tired, much like he had last year when he left Birdie and me at the Badala Park Hotel in Serrekunda, The Gambia.

I said to him and Birdie, "Wow! It surely is hot to be the twenty-first of December."

Turning to Mamadou, I asked, "Is it just that I'm excited, or is it hot?"

Birdie said, "I was thinking the same thing."

"Oh no, it is not hot here," he contradicted. "This is our winter season, and the temperature is just in the eighties."

"Just in the eighties?" I asked questioningly, "And I brought this heavy Brittany wool coat with me, which I definitely won't need if the temperature stays in the eighties."

"It is quite chilly here now," he countered, not realizing the depth of my observation.

Just then, our bags came around and Mamadou reached down to pull them off of the carousel.

"But look!" Birdie said as she scanned the crowd. "Even though the temperature is in the eighties, these people are all bundled and wrapped up in winter clothes, so I guess they're cold."

"I guess so," is all I could say as we turned away from the carousel.

In his usual take-charge manner, Mamadou commanded, "Follow me."

Obediently, Birdie and I followed him like two little girls. Even though he was carrying our luggage, he was taking those long strides that had me struggling to keep up with him.

I reached in my purse and got out my handkerchief to wipe the sweat from my face and bewailed, "I'm going to burn up in the clothes I brought with me if it's as warm outside as it is in here now, and it's about one o'clock in the morning. But this time, I brought a lot of Gaines's handkerchiefs with me so I can wipe the sweat."

When we arrived at the front door to leave the terminal, I was glad to see Madame Gueye and the others in a group there waiting for us. Mamadou turned and faced Birdie and me and declared explicitly, "You will be riding with Madame Gueye since you will be staying with her as her houseguests."

We bade the others farewell for the time being.

To Birdie and me, Madame Gueye said, "Come with me."

She led us to her car which was parked alongside the curb. The men loaded our baggage into the trunk.

As we waited for them, my mind traveled back to the occasion of dinner with Madame Gueye and her family. That had been one of the highlights of my Pilgrimage, and it had endeared me to the intimacy of my Motherland. Having gone on my Pilgrimage as an empty vessel, at that point I'd felt filled to overflowing.

Mamadou's brother came around to the side of the car where Birdie and I were standing. He assured us, "While you are here, if there is anything I can do to help make your stay more pleasant, please be sure to let me know."

We thanked him. Mamadou opened the front passenger door. I got in. He then opened the back door and ushered Birdie in. Mamadou and his brother got into the back seat with Birdie in the middle.

With everyone seated, Madame Gueye started the motor, and we took off to the entrance of the same expressway that Birdie and I had ridden when we left the airport terminal just about a year and a half before. I took a good look around, and even though it was dark, I recognized some of the same buildings as landmarks.

As we rode, Madame Gueye said, "I am happy that you accepted my invitation to be my houseguests. I hope you will be comfortable in my home while you are here."

I couldn't resist replying, "Oh, Madame Gueye, it is our distinct honor for you to have invited us to be your houseguests. I know we'll be comfortable in your home. We fully appreciate the fact that this will be an experience that I'm sure most African Americans visiting Senegal and Dakar in particular, will never have the opportunity to boast about. I will treasure sharing my experiences with my family and friends when I return to America."

Birdie added, "Madame Gueye, I've already bragged to my family and friends about our invitation to be your houseguests while we're here in Dakar. They all think this whole experience is just wonderful."

I glanced over at Madame Gueye. She was smiling admiringly as she drove along the expressway. Just then, we left the expressway and entered a section of highway with less traffic. That section led into the residential area. Even though there was little or no traffic, I could feel that we were slowing down. I wondered why. Gradually, Madame Gueye came to a complete stop.

Right in front of us, there stood a uniformed officer. He slowly walked over to the driver's side of the car. Madame Gueye rolled down her window, and he said something to her in Wolof. Without saying a word back to him, she reached over me and opened the glove box. She took out a small leather portfolio. When she opened it, I could see that she took out some papers and handed them to the officer. He took a cursory glance at the documents. He then walked around as if he were checking the perimeter of the car. He returned to the driver's side window and said something else to her. She answered in Wolof. He returned the papers to her. She returned the papers to the portfolio, reached over me and put the portfolio back into the glove box. She then drove off.

I wondered if she had stopped voluntarily, if this was a routine checkpoint, or if the officer had signaled for her to stop. Realizing that it really wasn't any of my business, I was too courteous to ask since she didn't volunteer to share the significance of the incident with us. She just drove on in silence.

Meanwhile, I looked around and thought I saw several cars following Madame Gueye's car. Mamadou broke the silence and reiterated that if there was anything we wanted or needed while we were in Dakar, just to let him know and he would see to it that we got it.

I said, "Thank you very much."

Birdie reinforced his offer by saying, "That's very kind of you. We'll surely let you know if there's anything we need you to do for us."

By that time, Madame Gueye was driving up in front of the house. Another car pulled up behind us. The timing was perfect, because as she turned into the driveway, the garage door opened and her husband and one of their sons were positioned to greet us.

A warm feeling swept through my bosom as someone opened the door for me to get out of the car. It was then that I realized that while Mamadou and his brother had ridden with us, others had followed Madame Gueye all the way home, supporting and protecting us after picking us up from the airport so that we three women would not be traveling alone. My heart filled with pride, reminding me of the love these brothers had for us and how they demonstrated that love by their actions.

"Welcome home! Welcome home! Welcome to our home!" the Gueye family members said in unison. All the while, Mamadou and his brother began unloading our luggage from the trunk of the car.

Madame Gueye led us into the foyer of the house. She directed the men to our room down the hall. Birdie and I followed.

When she opened the door and flipped the light on. I saw immediately that our room had twin beds. The top sheet and blanket were turned down.

Again she smiled and said, "I hope you'll be comfortable."

"We'll be very comfortable, Madame Gueye," we reassured her as she closed the door.

I whispered to Birdie, "This was probably the boys' room when they were both growing up and living at home,"

Situating her luggage under the window that faced the hall and the indoor/outdoor garden, Birdie said "Yes, I rather imagine it was. It looks like it."

I spotted an armoire or chiffonier in the corner of the room by the window.

"I'll be very comfortable as soon as I don't have to handle this wool coat in this heat. I don't even want to look at this thing," I said, stuffing my coat into an empty space in the back of the armoire.

Noticing what I was doing, Birdie added with a laugh "We won't need any coats here if the temperature stays like it is, and by now, it's the wee hours of the morning."

I noticed as we were situating our luggage, the curtains weren't moving. They weren't moving because no breeze was coming into that room from the indoor/outdoor garden.

We heard a soft knock on the door. Birdie opened the door, and there stood Madame Gueye. She was holding a circulating fan.

She was smiling as she came in. She said, "I see that you were sweating. I thought you would be more comfortable if you had a fan in your room."

We both thanked her as she plugged it in for us. She then invited us into the living room. We followed her out of the bedroom and down the hall. Before we entered the living room, we copied her tradition. At the doorway, we slipped out of our shoes.

I caught a familiar whiff and said, "Oh, Birdie, I think I smell some of that delicious tea we had when we were here before."

Surely enough, as we entered the living room, there on the floor beside Monsieur Gueye's lounge chair, was a small charcoal burner that he was attending. He was brewing the tea for us.

Birdie sat on the sofa beside Madame Gueye, and I sat in the matching over-stuffed chair.

As Monsieur Gueye was getting ready to serve us our tea, Mamadou and his brother said they were leaving.

But before they left, Mamadou informed us, "I have stocked your room with some extra provisions for snacking. I hope they will help to make you happy, but if there are other things you wish, let Madame Gueye know. She will tell me, and I will get them for you."

We bade them good night as they assured us that we would be gathering the next day at Mamadou's house where we would meet his bride-to-be.

Birdie and I made ourselves comfortable, and her husband served us tea.

The TV was on. There was a Senegalese cultural event being televised. Near the end of the telecast, a segment of the program included a short interview with a young local talent show participant. To my delight, I recognized the interviewer.

"Isn't that gentleman the curator at the Slave House?" I asked.

"Oh! You recognize him? Yes," Madame Gueye replied, "he is the principal curator at Le Maison des Esclaves on the Island of Goree. His name is Joseph Ndaye."

I told them, "He's the gentleman who delivered the lecture at the Slave House when Mamadou took us there when we were on our Pilgrimage last year."

I looked over at Monsieur Gueye. He was smiling proudly. It appeared to me that he got the gist of our conversation, even though he didn't speak English.

At a lull in our conversation, I asked, "Madame Gueye, is there a church within walking distance of your home where Birdie and I could attend a worship service on Sunday?"

"Yes," she was quick to reply. "There is a Catholic church not too far from our home. You do not have to walk. I will take you."

Silently I reflected on the fact that neither she nor Mamadou used contractions in speaking English as we African Americans did.

By the time the TV program ended, Birdie and I said good night to Madame Gueye and her husband, excused ourselves, went to our room, and got ready for bed.

Again, there was that soft knock on our door. Madame Gueye came in and informed us, "I'll be leaving for work in the morning before you get up, but my house helpers will be here and at your service. They will serve you breakfast whenever you want."

As she was saying that, she said to Birdie, "Here is a key to your room."

"Thank you for everything, Madame Gueye. Good night, and we hope you rest well," we said to her as she closed the door.

I didn't pay any attention and assumed that Birdie put the key in her purse.

I lay awake for quite a while recapping the events of the day. I took out my portfolio and made a few quick notes in my journal, crawled under the sheet and finally fell asleep.

Our First Full Day in Dakar

Early the next morning, I was awakened by what I could only describe as an eerie, haunting mantra, except it wasn't set to music. It sounded as if it were far away, and yet it sounded as if it were close by. It was mystifying yet welcoming, and the echo resounded. As a matter of fact, it is hard to describe it in words. But I can hear it right now as I sit here, writing. Later, I learned that it was the daily "call to prayer" or "call to worship." I admitted to myself that I was excited, but I soon went back to sleep.

Close to two o'clock in the afternoon when we casually emerged from our room, Madame Gueye's house helpers greeted us. Neither of them spoke any English, but they apparently understood that we were up for the day and that we would like something to eat.

As soon as we sat down at the table which was situated at the far end of the foyer just next to the indoor/outdoor garden, they promptly served us cut-up melons, that indescribably delicious French bread with butter, coffee, and juice. I had another emotional moment that reminded me of our first visit to Madame Gueye's home.

Soon after we started eating, one of Madame Gueye's sons greeted us and joined us at the table. He appeared to be in his late teens. I was impressed by the fact that he voluntarily sat down at the table with us older African American women, especially realizing the wide generational gap between him and us. Beside the fact that he chose to sit down and talk with us, I was even more impressed that he was fluent in English. He elicited conversation, and it flowed spontaneously. His countenance revealed that he was comprehensively interested in what we had to say. We asked him questions, and he answered openly. In fact, he stated that he had aspirations to study in America. I was even more impressed by his next statement. He said that if he were granted a student visa for an opportunity to study in America, when he completed his studies, he intended to return to Senegal to share his acquired knowledge and expertise with his people for the betterment of

25

his country. Judging from the substance of his conversation, it was obvious to me that he was wise, intelligent, well-grounded, and goal oriented.

Off and on while we all sat there, one of the girls would check the table and replenish our breakfast foods. At one point, he said something to her in Wolof, and she brought a teapot with steaming hot water to the table for refills of tea.

After breakfast, he told us, "I have enjoyed talking with you, and I will see you later. Now, I am going to see a friend who lives not far from here."

"It was good to talk with you, too," we said to him as he left the table.

Since we had finished breakfast, Birdie and I began going through the preliminary motions of getting ready to clear the table ourselves, but from their body language, the house helpers made it known to us that they would take care of everything.

Birdie suggested, "Jane, let's take a walk."

I told her, "That's a good idea. That way, we'll be able to see some of the surrounding area in the daylight since when we were here before, it was almost dark when we arrived for dinner."

"We'll take our cameras and get some pictures," she added.

I took a good daytime look at the indoor/outdoor garden. It was even more of a novelty to me than it had been when I'd taken pictures of it on our first visit to their home. It seemed like the ideal point to begin our picture-taking. So just before leaving the house, both of us took pictures of the garden. As I focused on different angles, I realized that because it was dark when I had been there before, I hadn't really appreciated the uniqueness and full beauty of that feature of their home. As we were admiring the plants and flowers, one of the house helpers was watering some of the palms. The other one was clearing the table and taking dishes to the kitchen.

House Helper Tending Plants in Indoor/Outdoor Garden

As they went about their tasks, it became apparent to me that these girls were paid employees as house helpers for the Gueye household.

We went to our room to get our purses. On our way out, Birdie locked our bedroom door. We sauntered down the hall to the front door, closed it softly behind us, looked around the courtyard, took some more pictures, and then walked aimlessly out onto the sidewalk.

We stood there in front of the house, admiring the ambience of the setting and surroundings. It was a bright, sunshiny day. The sky was as clear as it could possibly be, and the air was fresh and clean. There was a slight but warm breeze; there was absolutely no chill in the air.

All of a sudden in sheer delight, Birdie cried out, "Just think, Mum Jane, here it is almost January, and I don't even need a sweater or jacket! I'm just lovin' this weather. I love it so much that I don't want to go back home where it's so cold."

"Well, just enjoy it while you can," I said, trying to calm her down.

With the sound of the front door closing, we looked around. The two house helpers came out. We greeted each other as they walked toward us. As is true with most Senegalese, by our being demonstrative, they both appeared to catch the gist of what we were saying to them, and they were able to respond in a way that we understood, too. Oh, how I wished I could have just sat down and talked with them in their language or in my English.

We motioned for them to join us, one on Birdie's side, and the other one on my side. We strolled along in the direction of a workshop that was across but down the street from the house.

Two tradesmen were quick to catch our attention, busy at work where they had set up an open-air shop on a vacant lot.

"Let's go over and see what they're doing," Birdie suggested.

"OK, let's," I agreed.

They saw us coming as we crossed the street, and as we approached them, they smiled at us. I think they recognized Madame Gueye's house helpers. We introduced ourselves to them, and they introduced themselves to us, saying *"Asalamua alikum!" "Asalamua alikum!"* (Hello! Hello!)

When we got close enough to talk, we greeted them, saying, *"Nangadef! Nangadef!"* (How are you? How are you?)

While Madame Gueye's house helpers were talking to them in Wolof, I was thinking, *Here I am, back in my Motherland where my people smile and greet each other with warmth, even though we don't know each other. It seems they're pleased to acknowledge that we have the same roots.*

I said to Birdie, "It appears that they're happy that we're coming over to visit with them. This reminds me of the statement that the curator made in answer to my question after the lecture at the Le Maison Des Esclaves on Gorée."

"Yes," she said, "but many times at home when I pass African Americans on the street, they obviously avoid eye contact, as if they're denying the fact that we have the same origin. I'm sure you've experienced that."

"Yes, regretfully, I have. It's despicable and disappointing," I replied.

Our attention was drawn to the clip-clop of what sounded like hooves. As I looked around, a young man perched high on the seat of a donkey-drawn cart was rolling toward us. As he got closer, we waved at him. He smiled and waved back. There was little or no traffic on the street, so we were able to get a good snapshot as he passed by. The bed of the cart was loaded with what looked like straw, leaving only a small space for his seat up front.

We told the workmen we were Madame Gueye's houseguests from California and Ohio. Their good spirit emanated in their smiles and nods. When I thought seriously about it, I realized that we really didn't need to go through all that. There wasn't any doubt in my mind that they saw us come out of her house, and then when the girls joined us, their circumspection gave them more than an inkling that we were guests of the Gueye family. We asked them what they were doing, and they showed us their finished product. They were making what looked to me like, briquets of charcoal, made from some kind of raw material. They appeared pleased that we showed an interest in what they were doing.

Not being able to speak their language, I couldn't find out what the raw material was, but it looked like some kind of coal. However, it wasn't the kind that we used to put in our furnace to heat our house back in Iowa when I was a child. Also, it seemed that from the quantity of their product, there must have been a substantial demand, which justified their being engaged in the business. Behind them, there was a huge stockpile of the product. I wondered how they secured the supply from thievery after dark.

Before we left their work space, we took pictures with them and thanked them for spending a little time with us by saying, *"Jerejef! Jerejef!"* (Thank you! Thank you!) We strolled along the side of the street opposite Madame Gueye's house and took more pictures of some of the people who passed by. Some of them were students either going to class or coming from class. I assumed they were students, because they were weighted down with backpacks. Meanwhile, the girls left us and went back to the house. Apparently, they had more house chores to complete before the Gueye family returned.

Even though we were actually in Dakar itself, it seemed to me that we must have been on the outskirts of town. It was comforting just being there, looking around, taking pictures, and soaking up the serenity and peacefulness of the neighborhood.

Shortly, we saw Madame Gueye pulling into the driveway. We turned around to go back to the house. She hopped out of the car, and we joined her as we all walked into the house together. Soon Monsieur Gueye came in. They slipped out of their shoes at the doorway and led us into the living room. Birdie and I followed suit, took off our shoes and seated ourselves on the sofa.

Monsieur Gueye said something to her, and she in turn asked us about our flight from New York to Dakar on Air Afrique. (I didn't realize it then, but later, I found out why they were interested in knowing our reactions as to how the airline was functioning, the quality of service, or something like that.) As we talked, there was an atmosphere of peace and tranquility that permeated my soul, just being there with my people.

"I still can't believe we're back in Dakar so soon after our Pilgrimage," Birdie reminded all of us.

"And I'm still in a state of euphoria over the reason for our being here—the fact that Mamadou invited us to attend his wedding, a traditional African Islamic wedding," I told them.

In her typical elegant style, Madame Gueye called us to the dining area for a meal. We followed her lead and seated ourselves in Senegalese style on the floor around the large round platter of food. Their two sons and a cousin joined us.

Immediately, I recognized the menu of fish, rice, that delicious homemade tomato sauce, vegetables, and tasty French bread. We had cubed melons for dessert. There were no individual plates or eating utensils. Since we were served "family style," Birdie and I followed the tradition of our hosts and dipped into the serving platter with our right hand and ate with our fingers.

Madame Gueye asked us, "What did you do to occupy your time while I was away?"

It was rewarding to tell them about our getting acquainted with the workmen in the shop down the street. TheGueyes' expressions beamed with pride when we told them how we cherished the experiences of the afternoon. All the while, they were smiling and their exuberating expressions were heartwarming. It seemed to me that they were impressed with our adaptability and that we had observed so much. They complimented us on our resourcefulness.

After dinner, we retired to the living room for a short while and engaged in more conversation that centered on their Senegalese culture, heritage, and tradition. With emphasis, we were told, "It is preeminent that our heritage is to be preserved. Education is important so that our posterity has role models to emulate."

They told us that the example set by parents is to be revered and followed by children and that people follow the discipline of their leaders.

We touched lightly on the subject of drug abuse, particularly among youths. Out of this dialogue came the firm statement from Monsieur Gueye which his wife translated, "Drug addiction is not tolerated by Senegalese families. Drug addicts are ostracized from the family until their addiction is conquered. After that, the individual is welcomed back into the family unit."

After a while, Madame Gueye reminded us that Mamadou was expecting us to join him at his house to spend the evening with him and his family.

We agreed, and she left the room to go get the car. When she backed the car out, Birdie and I hopped in.

Along the way, I recognized familiar sights and sounds. Most of the ladies were elegantly dressed in bright-colored garments and headpieces to match. Such a signature of tradition instilled deeper respect in me for my ethnic identification with my motherland—Africa.

Some of the people were dressed in native garb, but I noticed that some of them were dressed in Western attire. When I pointed this out to Madame Gueye, she said, "Many youngsters dress in T-shirts and jeans. It is mostly the young people who dress in that casual, laid-back style."

Our route took us through the main residential area of that section of Dakar. As we rode, I thought about that night a year ago when we'd left Madame Gueye's house after dinner. It was late at night. For some reason, I remembered that in the darkness of that night, there were lots of people out and about and still doing business in the little shops and establishments along both sides of the streets. I also remembered that even though the streets were dimly lit, I didn't feel ill at ease because of it.

This time, there was lots of foot traffic in the streets as people were going about their business. As we rode along, every now and then, Madame Gueye would honk her horn and wave at someone she knew if they didn't wave at her first. Usually, they waved at her before she spotted them and had a chance to wave. It was obvious to me again that she was well-known and well-liked in her own community as well as in the outlying areas.

Soon we arrived in the area of Mamadou's house. There was no parking space in front so we parked around the corner and walked to the house. As usual, when we arrived, there were several family members present, as well as friends who had dropped in. I remembered the house and some of the pieces of furniture in the living room—the ultra comfortable over-stuffed sofa and chairs, the selected hues of the pieces of mahogany furniture, the French design sideboard, all were made of natural well-cured materials. There was a long hallway that seemed to isolate us from the hustle and bustle of food preparation, but not from the aroma. Something was cooking, and whatever it was, it smelled really good.

We sat down in the living room and a moment later, Mamadou's sister came out of the kitchen to greet us again; she had been at the airport to welcome us to Dakar. She was a married woman who looked to be in her mid-fifties. She had several children and some infant and toddler grandchildren who were present during most of the time. She gave us another big hug and welcome, and then she and Madame Gueye embraced and engaged in a brief conversation in their native tongue. I didn't know what they were saying, of course, and just hoped they weren't saying something negative about Birdie and me that we couldn't understand. Paramount to this, it was obvious to me that the two of them were good friends and that they loved each other very much.

Mamadou's sister returned to the kitchen, where I believe she was engineering preparation of the evening meal because I caught another whiff of onions, celery, and something else. My stomach growled even though I had eaten just a short while ago.

More friends and family drifted in. We were warmly greeted with, *"Asalamua alikum!" "Asalamua alikum!"* (Hello! Hello!)

Birdie and I beamed as we proudly and confidently spoke our limited Wolof response, *"Nangadef! Nangadef!"*

Those whom we hadn't met before introduced themselves to us. I explained that I lived in California, and Birdie explained that I was her mother-in-law. She pointed out that she lived in Ohio. They seemed fascinated by the fact that we lived so far apart but were in-laws. At that point, it was obvious to me that they were knowledgeable about the geography of the continent of North America—probably more so than some Americans—but ill informed about the necessity of living wherever employment was available for African Americans in the United States.

Soon, one of Mamadou's English-speaking brothers came in and introduced himself. He too was friendly and conversant. Like Mamadou, he was tall, handsome, and articulate. He asked us if everything was going all right since we'd been there.

"Of course," we replied, "Everything is just fine."

By both of us being married women, I wanted to make it clear to everyone that we weren't there looking for male companionship, so I promptly clarified our relationship, marital status and the significance of our presence in Dakar by informing everybody, "We're honored that Mamadou invited us to attend his wedding. We're exceedingly happy to have been able to come for his very special event."

Those remarks seemed to please all of them.

To get a breath of fresh air, Birdie and I went out on the veranda. While we were watching the comings and goings in the street below, one of Mamadou's cousins came out to greet us. She was a rather heavy-set woman who looked to be in her late forties. She was dressed in a stunning native garment with matching head-wrap. She approached us, welcoming us to Dakar. Almost simultaneously, Birdie and I both complimented her attire. It was a two-piece, ankle-length garment made of a colorful African print material with stylishly large, puffed sleeves. Birdie took a snapshot of her. I could read from the expression on the cousin's face that she was flattered as she gave Birdie a big hug.

Without our asking, she insisted on letting us try on her outfit.

Right out there on the veranda, she painstakingly began undressing and encouraged us to take off our outer garments. (It was a two-story house and the veranda was high above street level, so no one could see up there.) As we did that, she carefully adorned Birdie in the garment and head-wrap. That gesture of love was so overwhelming, I couldn't resist saying, "Birdie I'm going to take a souvenir picture of you in that outfit." She handed her camera to me.

After I snapped the shot, she took off the outfit, and Mamadou's cousin carefully adorned me in her outfit."

Birdie returned the favor by saying, "Jane, as one of your souvenirs, I'm going to take a picture of you in the same outfit as one of your souvenirs."

We changed back into our own clothes, and Mamadou's cousin got dressed. We all walked back into the living room to join the rest of the family and friends.

Moments later, Mamadou arrived hand in hand with his wife-to-be, Suweeyah Salih. Her mother followed close behind them. He introduced them to us, and since they were African American, we were able to relax and say, "How do you do? It's a pleasure to meet you. Congratulations and best wishes!"

Mamadou asked, "Mum Jane and Birdie, have you met everyone else in the house?"

We replied, "Yes, we've met everyone."

Several members of the family asked us detailed questions about traveling from America to Senegal. Mamadou's niece—his oldest sister's youngest daughter who also speaks English—translated questions from them to us and our answers to them. It was apparent that they were curious as to the procedure—requirements for passports and visas, mileage from our homes to Dakar, and our previous international travel experiences.

Shortly, she left the room. After a few minutes, Mamadou's sister and her youngest daughter brought out a large straw mat. They covered the mat with a white tablecloth. On the tablecloth, they set a large platter of food.

As is their custom, we all sat down on the floor around the platter and began eating "family style" again with our fingers in traditional Senegalese tradition.

Traditional Seating for Dish of the Country

Mamadou was explicit in educating us that we were dining on *tiebou dienne*, "the dish of the country."

After dinner, we were served "wine tea." Birdie and I were very familiar with the aroma. It was delicious and served steaming hot. Light conversation flowed for the next couple of hours. I noticed that after a while, there were only family members left in the living room, so I surmised that the friends had drifted out one by one.

Interspersed in the conversation, Birdie and I directed questions to Mamadou regarding traditions of the African Islamic wedding. We asked, "Will there be an exchange of rings at the ceremony?"

The reply was, "No, there will not be an exchange of rings. It is against our religion for men to wear gold. Instead, the groom will give the bride-to-be a ring, a dowry, and gifts of clothing."

"Will the wedding take place in the mosque?" I asked with purpose, hoping he didn't remember what he'd told me on the phone—that the wedding would take place in his home. And too, I was thinking of information I'd picked up somewhere along the way that women were segregated in the mosque.

But he did remember and promptly replied, "No, the wedding ceremony will take place right here in the living room of my home." He said no more about it.

Also, Birdie asked him whether there would be a "jumping the broom" spectacle as a part of the wedding ceremony.

He looked bewildered and replied, "No, that is not a part of it."

Birdie and I had been searching for a clue as to what to give the newlyweds as a wedding gift. (Unbeknownst to each other, we were having a meeting of the minds.)

We stayed a good while longer, and then we got up to leave for home. As we were walking out of the house to the car, we said good night to the family members and few remaining friends.

Back to Madame Gueye's House

Mamadou and his brother escorted Madame Gueye, Birdie, and me to the car which was parked around the corner from his house.

I observed again that Senegalese men were protective of women. They didn't let us walk to the car alone in the dark, and that's the reason they escorted us.

Birdie and I got in. Madame Gueye drove us to her house.

As we pulled up in front of her house, another car simultaneously pulled up behind us. It was Mamadou and his brother who had followed us to Madame Gueye's to be sure we got home safely.

As soon as we got inside, I said to Birdie, "I'm going to get out of these shoes and put on my house slippers."

We walked down the hall to our room. When we got to the door, Birdie reached in her purse for the key. Not finding it immediately, I could tell that she was embarrassed. She began searching surreptitiously, then frantically. She searched and searched, even emptying out the contents of her purse onto the floor. But she still couldn't find the key.

With a tone of desperation, she said, "I just don't understand. We haven't used the key since this afternoon when I locked the door before we left to peruse the neighborhood."

By that time, Mamadou and Madame Gueye were standing at our sides. Madame Gueye didn't seem to be the least bit disturbed. She just walked away. When she returned, she smilingly handed another key to Birdie.

In his take-charge manner, Mamadou took the key from Birdie and said firmly, "I am going to make sure you do not lose this one."

He painstakingly attached the key securely to the hardware of her purse. We all had a big laugh at the creative way he demonstrated his inveterate nature and treated us like we were two little kids whom he had to look after.

Meanwhile, I got a whiff of that sweet, nutty, subtle aroma-like incense.

Monsieur Gueye was preparing tea for us. We all joined him in the living room, and while we sat sipping our tea, we drifted into conversation about the political climate of Senegal. In conclusion, we were told that Senegal had a democratic form of government that brought back stability to the country.

Madame Gueye disappeared from the room for a few minutes.

When she returned, she brought out two beautiful nearly identical garments. One was white and one was a rust color. They were one-piece, slightly longer than ankle-length dresses.

She gave the rust-colored one to Birdie and the white one to me. Secretly, I wished it had been the other way around since rust is one of my favorite colors. I didn't want to appear ungrateful, so I didn't say anything about it.

"What is this style of gown called?" I asked Madame Gueye.

Carefully enunciating, she answered, "It is called a *bou-bou.*"

"Jerejef! Jerejef!" ("Thank you!" "Thank you!") Birdie and I exclaimed almost simultaneously.

Her expression beamed as we said that to her in Wolof.

I asked her, "And while I think of it, Madame Gueye, what is the Wolof name of the headdress that some of the Senegalese women wear?"

Very academically, she explained, "It is called a *moussa.*"

I said to her, "I notice that some women wear it and some women don't. Is there some significance?"

With the same academic emphasis, she explained, "If a woman is married, she can wear a *moussa.* If a woman is not married, she is not supposed to wear a *moussa,* but some women do."

We thanked her again for that enlightening information.

Shortly, we all said good night to each other after warm hugs.

Birdie and I went to our room. We sat on the side of our beds, recapping some of the events of the day. I told Birdie that I felt like a sponge. I had absorbed so much "heredity" from the closeness and fellowship with my African family that I no longer felt "adopted." I felt totally genetically connected in every respect.

I made some more entries in my journal, and then crawled into bed. But I lay awake for a long time, just thinking.

Sunday Morning Worship Service

I awakened with a start when the alarm went off. It seemed as if I had just gotten well into a night's sleep. Right away, I could hear that mantra in the distance. I lay there for a few minutes, but was anxious to get up and connect with my family.

"I'll go to the bathroom first, Birdie, so you can get a few more winks in," I offered.

"OK," she sleepily replied.

When we were up and dressed, Madame Gueye invited us to the breakfast table. I noticed that she was doing everything herself. Her helpers weren't officiating.

I asked her, "Is this your helpers' day off?"

She replied, "Yes. On Sunday, I give them the day off to be with their families."

We had orange juice, freshly baked French bread with butter and jelly, and piping-hot coffee. I ate a lot, because it had been quite a while since the meal we'd eaten with Mamadou's family and friends the evening before.

Madame Gueye had perfectly timed our breakfast and departure for church. So as soon as we finished breakfast, I went to my room to get the bag of school supplies I had brought from home. When I asked Mamadou what I should bring with me, he told me that school supplies would be most appropriate. I was quite sure I'd see Mamadou that day and would give the bag to him right away. We went into the garage to get into the car.

To our surprise, Madame Gueye couldn't get the car started, so her son immediately came out to help. Since the car was a Mercedes-Benz, I presumed that the family didn't drive that car very often which accounted for the difficulty in starting it. However, it took only a minute, and when he got it started, Birdie and I got into the back seat. I set the bag of school supplies on the floor at my feet.

There was a beautifully woven shopping basket laying there on the floor in the back. I thought to myself, *What a beautiful basket*. It had an ornate half-moon-shaped handle on it, and the body had an intricate pattern of different-colored straws woven throughout.

"This is another warm day here in Dakar," I said to Madame Gueye as she drove through a new development compound and pulled up in front of a Catholic church.

Before we got out of the car, Madame Gueye said, "The service will last about an hour. After the service, just stand outside at this same spot. I will be back to pick you up in an hour."

As soon as we got out, she drove off.

We walked up the steps. It was obvious to me that this edifice had just recently been built. When we got inside, I could see that the sanctuary was huge, with parts of the structure purposely open at the top. In other words, there was no ceiling. As I always sit near the front of a church, I led Birdie up the aisle to one of the front pews. I sensed that we were a few minutes early.

After we took our seats, I observed that the choirmaster was still busy with his pre-service duties.

On the hour, a priest dressed in full religious garb appeared through a velvet curtain. He stepped up to the lectern. I took a quick glance around, and from my vantage point, the sanctuary appeared to have nearly filled up since our arrival.

The service began. We were directed to stand for the invocation and then to be seated.

The choir sang hymns from a hymnal printed in Latin. While the choir was singing, I counted forty people in the choir. I was struck by the fact that there were more male singers than female singers, but the voices were well balanced with sopranos, altos, tenors, and basses. *Quite the opposite in America,* I thought, because usually there are more women than men in most church choirs. Their selections were written and sung in classical western European form, and the choirmaster directed the choir from his seat at the organ.

The litany was in English, led by the Caucasian priest with a heavy European accent. The ritual was not difficult to follow. In fact, I could relate to the crux of the message which was to contribute time and talent to one's community.

The priest recited a benediction in an unemotional, rote tone of voice. However, I fully appreciated the special occasion, because attending a church service had been high on my list of priorities to experience at some time while in Dakar. Having acquired that knowledge and spiritual uplift, I felt fulfilled as we walked down the aisle to the exit.

I was enchanted by the experience and thought this to be remarkable. I didn't know why I gave that any thought, except that there Birdie and I were—she a Baptist and I a United Methodist, both followers of the Christian religion—

attending Sunday service in a Catholic church in Dakar, Senegal, West Africa, where the predominant religion was Islam.

Following Madame Gueye's direction, Birdie and I headed for the pick-up point in front of the church. What timing! Just a couple of minutes after we got to our waiting point, she pulled up. We got in, and she pulled away from the curb.

She asked us what we would like to do for the rest of the day. We told her we'd like to go to Mamadou's house to fellowship with him and his family, and we hoped she'd be able to spend some time there with us.

She said she had hoped we wanted to do that, and since she purposely had not made any other plans for the day, she'd be happy to spend it with us, the Niang family, and friends.

She drove for what seemed to me to be quite a long way. And then when we got into Mamadou's neighborhood, we discovered that there were lots of shoppers in the immediate area. Again, she had to park around the corner from his house.

Getting out of the car, I picked up the bag of school supplies to take with me to give to Mamadou. At the same time, Madame Gueye reached in and picked up that beautifully woven basket from the floor of the back seat.

"What a beautiful basket," I said to her.

She smiled and said, "Thank you. This is one of my shopping baskets."

The three of us walked from around the corner to the house, weaving in and out among the townspeople as they browsed along the streets of the marketplace.

Sunday Afternoon and Evening with Madame Gueye at Mamadou's

Of course, there was an assembly of friends to greet us, and others came soon after we got inside. Shortly, Mamadou came in. Of course, then the socializing, conversation, and laughter escalated to "high C." There was no doubt that his charismatic personality just drew people to him and him to people, because right behind him came friends and family members.

Soon after he came in and Madame Gueye was comfortable that we had melded into the group, with that shopping basket on her arm, she said to Birdie and me, "I am going to do some shopping in the market but will be back in a little while."

While everyone was seated in the living room, I went out on the veranda for a breath of fresh air and to take a look around. The area and atmosphere was so ethnic that I decided to take some more pictures. I had a perfect vantage point from the veranda of the house and captured snapshots of the shopkeepers touting their wares to natives and tourists.

When I came back inside, I picked up the bag of school supplies, walked over to Mamadou, gave the bag to him and said, "Here are the school supplies you told me to bring with me. The bag contains pens, pencils, erasers, writing tablets, colored construction paper, and chalk for the chalkboard. I want you to take it to an elementary school and give it to the principal or headmaster. That person will be able to determine the pupils who will benefit the most from the contents."

With a broad smile, he said, "Mum Jane, I will do that as soon as I can. *Jerejef! Jerejef!*" In return, I thanked him in advance for carrying out my instructions.

As I returned to my seat, I got a good whiff from the kitchen. My salivary glands came alive, and my stomach began to growl.

In a few minutes, Mamadou returned to the living room, came over to me and said, "Mr. Badiane told me to ask you and Birdie if you would accept an invitation to dine with him and his wife tomorrow (Monday) evening at their home."

Right away, I remembered the name and asked him, "You mean Mr. Badiane of Africa Connection Tours?"

"Yes. Yes." he answered.

"Oh, that would be wonderful, and we graciously accept their invitation," I replied with sheer delight.

Just as he turned away, it dawned on me that I should ask him an all-important question, so I called out to him, "Mamadou, Mamadou, how will we get to Mr. Badiane's home?"

Walking back to me, he assured me, "Don't worry, Mum Jane. Mr. Badiane will notify Madame Gueye to arrange transportation from her home to his home and back to Madame Gueye's on Monday evening."

"*Jerejef! Jerejef,*" I exclaimed with glee, and all the while I was thinking, *What an honor. The president and chief executive officer of the leading travel agency in Dakar, Africa Connection Tours, has invited me to dinner at his home. I can't wait to tell Birdie.*

I reflected on the propitious statement Mr. Badiane had sent to me when I wrote and published, *A Pilgrimage to Senegal and The Gambia, West Africa.* Again, my heart filled with pride, and yet I felt humble.

When I told Birdie, she became ecstatic. It was as if she had been keyed up with something. "Mum Jane, just think, we're invited to be guests of another celebrity in Dakar and the wedding hasn't even taken place yet," she said to me.

Joining in her excitement, I said, "Right. We came here for the wedding and have already been invited out to have dinner in the home of another Senegalese family. I just can't wait to tell everybody back home."

I guess we were strutting like two peacocks when we came back into the living room where all the folks were talking at the same time. But as we entered, the conversation lulled, and their attentions turned to us. I guess our expressions and body language conveyed the message that something special had happened for us.

They asked, "What happened?"

As an explanation, Mamadou translated for them, "Salif and his wife have invited Mum Jane and Sister Birdie to be dinner guests in their home on Monday evening."

Mamadou's brother asked, "Mr. Salif Badiane of the travel agency?"

"Yes!" Birdie and I exclaimed simultaneously, interrupting Mamadou.

"Oh, that is very nice," he said with a broad smile.

With a confident stride, I noticed that Mamadou left the room. He returned shortly, escorting his bride-to-be and her mother into the living room. We all greeted them.

Just then, I noticed that family members were bringing out a large straw place mat and tablecloth. They spread them in the middle of the floor. I knew then that a meal had been prepared and was about to be served. I had trouble controlling my salivary glands from overproducing and could only hope that nobody heard the loud, embarrassing hunger growls in my stomach.

Family members and friends began seating themselves in Senegalese style around the dinner platter. Birdie and I followed suit and positioned ourselves on the floor with them.

As if she had timed her return from shopping in the market, Madame Gueye joined us on the floor around the platter. Of course, Birdie and I followed the lead of our hosts by taking food from the serving platter with the fingers of our right hands. Oh, how I wished I could have washed my hands.

Tiebou Dienne (the dish of the country) which contained mother fish, rice in tomato sauce, and grilled onions was served, along with French bread, butter, watermelon for dessert, mixed-flavored punch and coffee.

For the benefit of all persons present, I poured out my heart but directed my sentiment to Madame Gueye, "This experience reminds me of the heartwarming fellowship you and your family extended to Birdie and me, along with the scrumptious meal that you served us in your home when we were in Dakar on our Pilgrimage. Somehow, I just know that everyone is not privileged to enjoy experiences such as these. I also know that these times were meant for me to treasure. It is most touching to be able to connect with my ancestors through your traditions. I believe that these experiences are a part of my destiny."

I felt proud when Madame Gueye translated my sentiments. I could read from the expression on everyone's faces that they were touched by my remarks. Everyone ate heartily, and I had to restrain myself from eating ravenously.

One by one we finished eating. The remains left on the platter were taken away. Shortly, I got a familiar whiff of that charcoal-brewed beverage. Soon, cups of the piping hot wine tea were served to each of us. It tasted so good that I had to be careful not to slurp it.

When we finished our tea, Mamadou asked, "How about going to the marketplace?"

Birdie and I said we'd like to go. So, Mamadou, Suweeyah (Mamadou's bride-to-be), her mother, Birdie and I all left the house, headed in that direction. We walked only a short distance and there it was. I can only describe the market as a virtual emporium where merchants, young and old, had a myriad of durable and edible goods and commodities on display for sale. All of the merchants looked African.

Of course, I knew the merchants would be very aggressive toward us African Americans in their approaches for us to buy their wares. Realizing this, I pulled Mamadou aside and asked him to review the exchange rates of Senegalese currency for me.

He instructed me in his pedagogical, authoritative tone of voice, "Mum Jane, just remember that one dollar equals five hundred CFAs, two dollars equals one thousand CFAs, five dollars equals twenty-five hundred CFAs, ten dollars equals five thousand CFAs, and twenty dollars equals ten thousand CFAs."

"But Mamadou, I can't remember all that all of a sudden," I said to him, mournfully.

"I will be with you when you make a purchase, so do not worry about it, Mum Jane," he said consolingly.

We caught up with the others who were strolling along just ahead of us. Everywhere on long display tables were bolts of varying colors and designs of fabrics. Ready-made garments—*bou-bous* and *dokcats*—were hanging from long rods. Scarves, beads, sandals, jewelry, incense, charcoal, and embroidered cloths were artfully and conspicuously displayed, as well as carved wooden figurines and other objects of art. The sand paintings caught my eye as well as what looked like papier-mâché masks, small home furniture items, and more—all too numerous to recollect at the moment.

We walked and browsed, made our purchases and left the marketplace.

"I only wish I could have made more purchases, but my concern is about being able to transport any more baggage back to America," I told the group as we left to go back to Mamadou's house.

Soon after we got back, Mamadou explained another cultural tradition, taking us next door to meet more members of his family.

We commented that he did, indeed, have a very large family. He immediately seized the opportunity to further educate us by telling us that all Senegalese are a part of his "family."

Of course at all times, I was anxious to totally absorb any and all of their culture. So of course, we let him take us over there.

Next door, we were warmly welcomed. Even though Birdie and I couldn't communicate in words, it appeared to me that they felt honored that Mamadou had brought us to meet and greet them. Soon others drifted in to meet Mamadou's wife-to-be, her mother, Birdie and me, Mamadou's adopted family from Ohio and California, USA. While there, we were served fruit punch and colas. Mamadou kept up a steady flow of conversation as if he hadn't talked with them for a long while.

At that hour of the night and after such a full day, we bade everyone good-bye and told Madame Gueye that we were ready to go home.

Mamadou and his brother followed Madame Gueye as she drove us home. I was so tired that as soon as I got there, I said goodnight to everyone.

Birdie and I retired to our room, anticipating happenings of the next day.

The Unveiling of Our Gowns

When we returned to our room after breakfast, as if we had been reading each other's minds, we shared our ideas for a wedding gift for the bride and groom. We both agreed that the most appropriate and practical gift would be the price of the bridal suite at the Hotel Sofitel Teranga in downtown Dakar. We put our money in an envelope. Birdie tucked it away in her purse.

As we came out of our room, we met Madame Gueye coming down the hall. We all hopped in the car, and Madame Gueye took us to Mamadou's house. When we got there, as usual, the house was already teeming with activity. Some members of the household were cooking, because I could smell onions, celery, and bell pepper frying. It was a familiar aroma, because I use the same combination of vegetables in some of my favorite recipes. It wasn't long before the house was again full of family and friends. They all greeted one another as if they hadn't seen one another for a long time. But it hadn't been that long, because I recognized most of them as having been at his house just the day before. They were all together—laughing, talking, eating, and having fun.

Mamadou came in and insisted that Birdie and I go down into his quarters to view our gowns. I could see how anxious he was to show them to us. At last, we were going to feast our eyes on our gowns. I figured the tailor had just finished making them.

With every step, I was wondering, "*Will I be able to fit into my gown? How is it made? What color is it?*" My mind was whirling as we approached his quarters.

I think I was holding my breath when he pointed to where our gowns were auspiciously hanging from what looked like a coat tree. But they were covered up.

He slowly and ceremoniously unveiled our gowns.

As he lifted the cover, I was astounded and said, "Mamadou, they are beautiful, just beautiful. They are not only gowns; they're outfits."

The outfits were exactly alike. The material was shiny rayon. The color was majestic purple. The design of the outfit was a long, ankle-length *bou-bou*. There

46

was a gold design embroidered on the hemline. There was a matching pair of pants that were to be worn under the *bou-bou*. The pants had the same matching gold design embroidered at the bottom on the outside of the pant legs.

"They're simply beautiful. They're so regal. I'll be proud to wear it at your wedding and also later in America," Birdie exclaimed. "They're simply beautiful! We'll take them home to Madame Gueye's with us tonight."

Mamadou promptly replied, "No, you may as well leave your gowns here, and then you can change into them when you get here tomorrow morning, because I want you to be here at ten o'clock."

"OK, then that's what we'll do," we both agreed.

We thanked him for his kindness and thoughtfulness in having our gowns tailor-made.

We left his quarters and as we climbed the stairs to the living room, Mamadou said to Birdie and me, "Come with me. I want to take you up on the roof."

We followed him up the steep flight of stairs.

He continued, with excitement in his tone of voice, saying, "The wedding will be all day, and there will be about three hundred guests."

Birdie and I flashed a glance at each other.

With awe, I responded, "We're surely looking forward to your special day, Mamadou."

Up on the Roof

By that time, we were at the top of the second flight of stairs leading to the roof. There in plain view, were five sheep. They were being attended by a shepherd.

Mamadou was quick to point out that there was one sheep unlike the others. With a distressed look and scowl on his face, he said, "I do not understand that sheep. What is the matter with him? He is just recalcitrant," he wailed, still pointing to that one unruly sheep.

With firmness but gentility, the shepherd was trying to encourage it to conform to some semblance of communal living among the other sheep. The shepherd was struggling, but with no apparent success. It was obvious that that sheep's behavior was just obstinate.

Having gotten a full survey of the logistics and size of the house from top to bottom, Birdie and I used our body and sign language between us and communicated that this would be the appropriate moment to present Mamadou with our wedding gift.

Birdie handed the envelope to Mamadou.

His eyes sparkled; he smiled as he took the envelope. He didn't open it, but looked straight into our eyes, put his arms around us and hugged us, as he exclaimed, *"Jeredef! Jeredef!"*

By that time, it was late in the day, and I was tired and weary. I think Madame Gueye sensed my weariness and in her diplomatic tone, told us, "You'd better let me take you home, because very soon your driver will be arriving to take you to your dinner engagement."

"And tomorrow is the big day and a long day," I said to Birdie.

Friends and family were still comfortably sitting in the parlor. They were absorbed in some African cultural enrichment program on television. I wished I could have stayed long enough to watch it with them, but weariness had set upon me.

"We're ready to go whenever you're ready to take us," Birdie said to Madame Gueye.

We all said good-bye.

As usual, it took several more minutes for Madame Gueye to finish her conversation with Mamadou's sisters and brothers who were still there.

Dinner with the Badianes

Finally, she took us to her car, and as we rode home, I admitted, "I'm really tired." But I didn't dwell on that, because we still had a dinner engagement to look forward to—dinner at the home of the president and chief executive officer of Africa Connection Tours, Mr. Salif Badiane.

As soon as we got to Madame Gueye's house, we excused ourselves, went to our room and made a quick change for dinner. While we were changing, I could hear a lively conversation in the foyer. At the same time, Madame Gueye called out to us that our driver had arrived to drive us to the Badianes' home.

When we came out into the foyer, she reminded us that the driver who had been sent to drive us was an employee at Mr. Badiane's travel agency. She identified him as the gentleman who met us at the airport, got us processed through immigration, transported us, and got us registered into the Sofitel Teranga Dakar Hotel the night we arrived on our Pilgrimage. Sure enough, I recognized him. It was Suryec. Obviously, he recognized us, too.

He ushered us to the car and opened the back door, and we got in. He got behind the wheel, and we took off. We rode for quite a while into a totally unfamiliar area. But soon, he announced that we had arrived. He got out and opened the back door for Birdie and me. All the while, I marveled to myself that we were receiving such royal treatment and service. But I was too proud to reveal what I was thinking, so I didn't say anything for fear he'd know that I wasn't accustomed to such grandiose attention. He walked us to the door and waited until Mr. Badiane answered. As soon as we walked into the foyer, Suryec disappeared.

Immediately upon entering, Mr. Badiane introduced us to his wife. I introduced Birdie to Mr. Badiane as the person who had written that propitious statement that I acknowledged in my book, *A Pilgrimage to Senegal and The Gambia, West Africa*.

He and his wife ushered us into their sitting room. After being seated, he asked us if we would enjoy an appetizer before dinner. Of course, we accepted and began to make light conversation. No sooner had we had finished our appetizer that his wife announced that dinner was served in the dining room. They led us there.

I was quick to notice that the table was set exactly as I would have set my table in my own dining room.

We had individual place settings with linen napkins, the dinner menu was contained in serving bowls, and the meat was on a platter in the center of a linen table cloth.

As soon as we sat down, our conversation resumed. We learned from them that they saw many social and economic similarities, as well as differences, between the African and African American cultures.

"I think that's a profound observation. Thank you for sharing that with us," I said to them as I served my plate.

After a brief silence, Birdie shared her observation, saying, "I was surprised that there were so many African Americans on our flight from New York to Dakar at this time of year. And I noticed that almost all of them were carrying large stuffed animals and the like,"

He told us that during the Christmas season, African Americans visited many different countries on the continent. Of course, they brought products from America as gifts to friends and relatives, but especially to friends and relatives in West Africa.

He went on to say, "At this time of the year, the travel and tourism business flourishes in all of West Africa, not only in Senegal and The Gambia."

I thought this was the opportune time, so I ventured to ask, "How do you observe Christmas Day in Senegal?"

He gave a quick, brief answer, stating, "Our observance is not commercialized as it is in America."

I didn't quite know what to say or how to diplomatically further probe his answer about other ways in which their observance of Christmas differed from the American observance, so I thought it was best to say nothing more about it.

It surprised me when he told us that not only some African Americans but also other Americans have the misconception that Africa is a country. He was explicit in informing us that Africa is the second largest of the seven continents.

However, he was gracious in saying that as travel had become more common the entire world population had become more erudite and had learned that Africa was a continent and that each country was unique unto itself with its own culture, heritage, and tradition.

He changed the subject and went on to say, "But we're so happy that you ladies were able to come back to Dakar at this time of the year and most especially for Mamadou's wedding. I guess you know that Mamadou is our chief tour guide, and we regard him very highly."

To keep our conversation on an uncomplicated plane, I reiterated that Mamadou had extended a personal invitation to both of us to be with him on the day he was to be married. I made the specific statement, "We feel honored and special for him to have invited us, and so we made every effort to be here and spend this time with him. Also, it was another golden opportunity for us to be able to fellowship with members of our African families in Senegal and The Gambia."

Birdie added, "And as family, having been invited to be the houseguests in Madame Gueye's home was so very special."

Mr. Badiane responded, "Madame Gueye and Mamadou and all of us do indeed regard the both of you as family. You see, the African family is a social family and a domestic family."

His wife added, "The African family does not diminish. Instead, it grows. Therefore, when a special event occurs, the family must come."

"Of course, you know we're going to The Gambia the day after Christmas. We have family there, too," Birdie announced.

Mr. Badiane assured us, "Yes, I am aware that you have extensive travel arrangements through my agency, and we have charted your travel in every detail."

I was savoring that food with my senses of both taste and smell as I picked up just a hint of cabbage in the mixed vegetables served with chicken, and potatoes. It all tasted so good. I must say I particularly relished those potatoes, and the French bread was so fresh, it tasted as if it had just come from the ovens of a patisserie. I lavishly spread on the butter, repressing the morbid reality of my chronic hypercholesterolemia. And to top it off, we had ice cream for dessert. Oh well!

During a lull in the conversation, I reflected on the Badianes' statements about the African family. I guess it was a natural sentiment for me to share my thoughts and say, "I've internalized your statement that the African family does not diminish, but instead, it grows. And I've compared the two ideologies—yours and the fact that my own immediate biological African American family is getting smaller and smaller as the years roll by."

Mr. Badiane changed the subject and with an air of pride, informed us, "From time to time, I'm in the United States on business. Therefore, I know a lot of people in America. I always enjoy my time there."

I let no time elapse before saying, "Here and now, I wish to extend a warm welcome to you and your family to visit my husband and me whenever you're in California or anywhere near California. It would be an honor to have you as our houseguests."

Not wanting to intrude on the rest of their evening, and by then it was after ten o'clock, we informed the two of them that we needed to leave and get some rest for the next day—Mamadou's wedding day.

As we rose from our chairs and left the table, I said to them, "Thank you again for the pleasure of dining with you in your home. It has been more than a pleasure. It has been an honor. Your hospitality is typically Senegalese with the delicious meal and the pleasure of your company. You have afforded us another honor which I'm sure most African Americans will never have the opportunity or pleasure to experience,"

Standing in the vestibule, I asked them, "Will you be attending Mamadou's wedding tomorrow?"

"Oh yes! Oh yes!" they both replied in unison, but looked and sounded surprised that I even asked.

All in the same breath, his wife said, "Mamadou is one of our favorite people, and we'll surely be there to support him on his very special day."

As we bade them good night, Mr. Badiane turned to me and said, to my delight, "You are special, just as Mamadou described you. It is our pleasure to have had the privilege to meet you and show our hospitality. As a matter of fact, we now consider you to be a precious, recent addition to our family. And I want you to know that I thoroughly enjoyed reading your book, *A Pilgrimage to Senegal and The Gambia, West Africa.*"

I was overcome with emotion and stuttered out something, probably something unintelligible, but I did want them to know I felt blessed by their warm hospitality and demonstration of love.

It seemed that we had just announced that we should depart when our driver, Suryec, appeared in the doorway to take us back to Madame Gueye's. We said goodnight and told them we looked forward to seeing them the next day, the wedding day. As we followed Suryec to the car, they assured us that we would see one another then.

Suryec seated us, got behind the wheel and drove us home.

When we rode up to the front of the house, sleepily, I said sleepily to Birdie, "The ride back didn't seem as long as it seemed getting there."

"Right. Somehow, it never does, and I was thinking the same thing," she replied.

Back to Madame Gueye's

Suryec got out of the car, came around to the back door and let us out. He escorted us to the door where we were met by Madame Gueye. He bade us goodnight as Madame Gueye welcomed us back into their home.

As soon as we walked in, I caught that familiar aroma. Monsieur Gueye was preparing the wine tea treat. Madame Gueye led us into the living room. Of course, Birdie and I slipped out of our shoes and followed her as her husband welcomed us back.

We sat down on the sofa and caught the last part of a program centered around a traditional Senegalese baby-naming ceremony which was taking place on television. The program ended. Oh, how I wished we had seen all of it.

Within the next couple of minutes, Madame Gueye motioned to her husband, and asked us, "Would you like some libation?"

We answered, "Yes."

"And while I think of it, why is your libation served so frequently?" I asked.

Monsieur Gueye made a rather lengthy statement to his wife in Wolof, and she immediately translated to us that he'd said, "Serving and drinking the libation is a way of honoring our ancestors for their wisdom, culture, knowledge, courage, and self-discipline."

I got a little choked up, but said, "That is surely an emotional reminder and tribute to our ancestors."

As we sipped, we began sharing bits and pieces of our conversation at dinner in the Badiane's home. I shared with them the singularity of the experience of being a houseguest in the home of one of Mr. Badiane's agency employees and just having returned from being honored by him at dinner in his home.

The tea was calming, almost tranquilizing. And again, I realized that I was undeniably tired, worn-out, and now, sleepy.

Birdie was quick to say that our hosts, too, appeared to be tired, so we excused ourselves by saying, "It's very late, and all of us have a long day ahead of us tomorrow, so we must get some rest."

We exchanged good nights as we went to our room.

I was so tired, I sprawled out on my bed. I lay there for a moment, reminiscing about the events of the day.

Purposely, I sat upright for fear I'd fall asleep before I could make some significant notes in my journal. I surely didn't want to rely totally on my memory.

Mamadou's Wedding Day

When the alarm went off at seven o'clock, I wasn't ready to get up. But I was awakened by sounds of activity in and around the kitchen. I could hear that "call to worship" mantra in the distance.

Ready to start the day when we emerged from our room, our traditional continental-style breakfast was on the table and Madame Gueye welcomed us to be seated. Between us, we consumed the better part of a whole baguette of French bread with our juice and coffee. Her coffee always tasted so good that I picked up the can so I could read the label. Surprisingly, I was able to translate from my rusty college French that the words printed on the label, something like *sucré lait abrégé* translated to what we called "sweetened condensed milk" in America. So that's what made my coffee taste so good.

Birdie and I at breakfast

Excusing ourselves as Madame Gueye's house helpers began clearing the table, we went to our room to get ready to leave for Mamadou's house. We dressed in everyday casual clothes since Mamadou told us to leave our gowns at his house and to change into them after we went there.

"Bear in mind what Mamadou told us," Birdie reminded me as she spread up her bedding.

"What's that?" I asked her.

She reminded me, "Remember, he said he wanted us to be at his house by ten o'clock."

"Oh yes, I remember. But I'm sure Madame Gueye will get us there by that time," I assured her.

Just as we came out of our room, Madame Gueye came down the hall dressed in a beautiful frothy pale peach-colored chiffon African gown.

Facing her as she walked toward the front door, Birdie and I almost simultaneously complimented her outfit. Birdie paid her a special compliment by telling her, "That's a beautiful outfit you're wearing."

"And you look stunning in it," I said to her.

She smiled demurely and thanked us. "Are you ready?" she asked.

"Yes, we're ready," we both replied.

As we walked out the front door and headed down the street, she said, "We are going to take a taxi. There will be many people attending the wedding and lots of cars will be parked up and down the street, in front of and around Mamadou's house."

"OK, whatever you choose to do is fine with us," I said to her.

While walking, my special inner spiritual voice again reminded me that Mamadou had included me as family and invited me to attend his wedding. I felt humble. Also, I felt abundantly blessed. I thanked God for this special blessing and all of His countless others.

We walked, mostly in the streets, for what seemed to me to be quite a long distance. The streets are narrow but wide enough for automobiles, people, and animals. In fact, wherever we were going to catch a cab was much further than I had anticipated. Of course, a short walking distance to the Senegalese is not such a short walking distance to me. And Madame Gueye's gait was rather swift, or was it that I'm not as young as I used to be? It was probably some of both as I tried hard to keep up with her and Birdie.

All along the way, people young, old and all in between who were close enough to pass us, greeted Madame Gueye—and those in the distance, waved to her. I thought to myself, *Almost everybody knows Madame Gueye, and she knows almost everybody. But then, why are you surprised? She's a delightful person, and she's well-known in her community.*

As we slowed down on the last lap of our trek, she said, "I am going to take you by my husband's business on our way to get a taxicab."

Frankly, I hoped she was going to tell us that we'd arrived at a taxi stand to get our ride, but instead, we were just entering a small industrial area.

Sitting outside in front of a shop door was her husband. I immediately got the impression that he was expecting us, because as we approached, he stood up and smiled as he walked toward us. The two of them talked briefly, and then he hailed a taxi for us. As he opened the doors for us to get in, she explained that he'd be along later in time for the wedding. We hopped in, and the driver took off.

I consciously dismissed everything from my mind except for a primary thought, *Birdie and I are on a mission. I'm on my way to Mamadou's wedding.* I felt almost reverent.

When we arrived in the neighborhood, I realized that Madame Gueye was absolutely right to bring us in a taxi, because there wouldn't have been anywhere to park in the immediate vicinity. In fact, there were so many cars parked and so many people milling around, I asked her, "Why are these people here so early in the day?"

"This is a very special event, and these people are Mamadou's friends and family members who have been looking forward to this event from the very day they learned that he was getting married," Madame Gueye explained as we stepped out of the taxi. "Some of them have come into town from near and faraway villages to be with him. Lots of people know Mamadou, and he is loved and respected in Dakar."

Taking a quick glance at the entire area, I could see that nearby streets had been blocked off. An unmistakable aura of anticipated festivity permeated the air. I reflected on what Mamadou had told me over the phone before I left home, that he expected some three hundred people.

As I trotted along, Madame Gueye led us. Birdie was following right behind her, and as usual, I was bringing up the rear. I had to quicken my steps purposely so I could keep pace with them, because I didn't want anyone to step in between them and me until I got to the front door.

When we got there, I noticed that a canopy had been erected from the entrance of the house to the street. As I walked under it, I again had to control my emotions. I did my best, but still, my eyes welled up with tears of joy as we walked through the front door.

Of course, there were greeters in place to welcome us. When I saw them, I could envision Mamadou pointing his finger at whomever he had designated to greet us, and I could hear him giving emphatic instructions to family and friends to be at the front door to meet and greet Birdie and me (Sister Birdie as he calls her and Mum Jane as he calls me) when we arrived.

Madame Gueye led us as we climbed the stairs to let the family know that we'd arrived. As soon as we acknowledged all of them, we announced that we were going back downstairs to change from our everyday clothes to the gowns Mamadou had made for us to wear on this, his wedding day.

As soon as we got down, I knew that I wanted to get dressed as quickly as I could, because it was a really hot and humid morning. As soon as we were dressed, a family member ushered us back upstairs to the parlor.

When we walked in, I saw Mamadou seated on the floor at the feet of an elderly gentleman who was talking to him. Mamadou's countenance was prayerful and pensive. He was listening intently to what sounded to me like a lecture. The room was silent. Only the voice of the elder was audible. He and Mamadou were the only two people in the room when we were ushered in.

Birdie and I were led to two collapsible chairs situated side by side up front near the center of the room. I noticed that there were two more collapsible chairs also set up right beside the chairs where Birdie and I were directed to sit.

After we sat down, I surreptitiously took a quick look around and noted that the elderly gentleman was wearing white full-length African garb. Mamadou was wearing a brown rayon *bou-bou* with black braided trimming around the neck and down the front.

It seemed like we sat there in silence for a half hour or so in respect for the elder's monologue. At last, friends and family began to drift in—some alone, some in twos, some in threes, and some in fours, children accompanied by adults, other children ranging in age from babes in arms to toddlers, teenagers, young adults, and elderly men and women. I wondered how all of them could be seated in the room, but dismissed the thought from my mind, admitting to myself that it would be impossible. Yet, I noticed that no one attempted to occupy those two chairs that were set up—one next to Birdie and one next to me. So I presumed that they were being saved for Mamadou and his bride-to-be.

Finally, Mamadou's bride-to-be and her mother were slowly ushered into the parlor. They were seated in the two vacant chairs beside Birdie and me. Suweeyah was dressed in a beautiful floor-length white gown with gold braid embroidery around the neck and down the front. Her head was covered with a matching white and gold braid embroidered head-dress that resembled a veil worn back-ward. It was then that I realized why no one had occupied those two chairs.

At that point, a Senegalese man came over to us. He introduced himself as one of Mamadou's close friends. He spoke fluent English in a resounding, beautiful, low-pitched voice. We acknowledged the introduction.

He very clearly enunciated, "I have been designated by Mamadou to serve as your interpreter since the message will be delivered in Wolof." He went on to say that the gentleman who was to conduct the service was Mamadou's spiritual leader and that the ceremony was about to begin.

We thanked him.

He walked around us and stood directly behind our chairs.

As I sat there, I was absorbed in thought. Here I was in Dakar, Senegal, West Africa, and a part of the significance of the occasion—and particularly, the total experience—was that I'd been invited to witness the marriage of Mamadou, my *sama dome*.

At that point, the elder began delivering his message. Our interpreter began translating as guests quietly streamed into the parlor and sat in whatever seats were still available. Soon there were no more seats, so they stood along the walls. Others sat on the floor. Some were standing in the doorway and up and down the hall.

I observed that Mamadou was very emotional. In fact, he was tearful at times. He appeared to be listening intently as the spiritual leader began his liturgy in a forceful and authoritative voice. His voice projected extremely well. It almost sounded to me like he was lecturing to Mamadou. I must admit that I don't remember much of what he said, but I do remember our interpreter telling us that our beloved Mamadou Niang was stepping into marriage with full knowledge of the true meaning of a marriage. He emphasized that the structure of the African family rejected individualism but instead, purported powerful family relationships. He said that the two of them were blessed to have found each other and to be able to share their lives together. In this context, he accented his hope that Mamadou and his wife would be prolific and bring forth children to enlarge their families—not only their biological families but also the African family.

The spiritual leader was laudatory to Mamadou. He described Mamadou as a spiritual person and a man of deep-seated religious faith. He stated that Mamadou's religion was more than a belief. Rather, it was a fundamental way of life for him. He went on to say that Mamadou demonstrated his religious faith from day to day by his words, his actions, and his deeds.

All of a sudden, a female arose from her chair. In a loud, impetuous voice, she interrupted the lecture. From her body language, it seemed to me that she directed her verbal wrath toward another female seated on the floor not far from her. They were both dressed in elegant African attire, complete with matching *moussas*.

For the next thirty seconds, the two of them exchanged a heated dialogue. In addition to their body language, the inflection in their voices led me to believe that there was some kind of acrimony between the two and/or there was some objection to something that had been said. In fact, it was discernible to me that we were witnessing a latent embryonic verbal confrontation. Furthermore, it was noticeable to me that no one intervened or interrupted the two of them. Also, it was noticeable that none of that dialogue was translated for us.

The spiritual leader continued his monologue, and when he finished, he acknowledged the presence of us three other African Americans—Suweeyah's mother, Birdie, and me, Mamadou's other mother.

I leaned over and whispered to Suweeyah, "Are you married yet?"

She smiled bashfully, shook her head and whispered back, "I don't know."

Our interpreter leaned over and told us that Mamadou's spiritual leader asked if we had anything to say. I was astounded. I nearly fell off my chair but quickly gathered up my composure. Since he asked, I felt duty bound to make some kind of comment. Therefore, I introduced myself as having been adopted by Mamadou as his *sama yaye* (other mother), and I said that I considered it a blessing that he had invited Birdie and me to his wedding. I then offered a short prayer.

Then, Mamadou and his spiritual leader got up and walked out of the room. Other males followed the two of them. Those other males were all dressed in white African garb.

Again, I leaned over and whispered to Suweeyah, "Are you married yet?"

She smiled modestly, shrugged her shoulders, and whispered back again, "I don't know."

Several family members and friends rose from where they were sitting and made remarks in Wolof. Our interpreter told us that they were offering words of congratulations and best wishes to Mamadou and his bride. Suweeyah remained seated there with us.

As the group began to disperse, again I asked Suweeyah, "Are you married yet?"

Again, she smiled demurely, shrugged her shoulders, and answered, "I don't know."

A voice inside me said, *Well when will she know when she's married? It seems to me Mamadou would have joined her, embraced her, kissed her, or done something to her. But he has left the room with his spiritual leader and all those other men.*

I caught myself and looked around the room because my thoughts had been so lucid, I wondered if they had been audible. No one was looking at me, so I guess they hadn't heard what I was thinking.

Again, I had to repress stereotyping this wedding experience in comparison to my North American wedding experience.

Just then, Mamadou's sister came to us and invited Birdie, Suweeyah, her mother, and me to join her. We got up and followed her. She led us down the stairs and out of the house to be seated under the canopy. As we got closer and closer, I could hear conversation, laughter, and loud recorded music. It was African music.

A large group of women were already congregated there under the canopy. The faithful and ever-present Madame Gueye joined us. The four of us were ushered to choice seats up front for our comfort.

Noticeably, there were no men in the gathering under the canopy—just women. By the time we got there, some of them had already begun dancing. Others were seated, clapping their hands, waving their arms in the air, and keeping time with the music with their feet.

On the far perimeter of the area, I saw a long procession of men all dressed in white African garb. They appeared to be marching, and it looked as if they were in single file.

I asked Madame Gueye, "Look over there. Where are those men going?"

She explained emphatically, "They are going to the mosque to pray. When they come back, Mamadou and Suweeyah will be 'married'."

In awe, all I could say was, "Oh!"

In the meantime, I noticed that Suweeyah had disappeared. I hadn't seen her leave. (I learned later that it was the custom for her to change her clothes at that point. So that's what she had gone to do.)

Again, I had to remind myself to reprogram my mind to think in terms other than my exposure to the most common Western custom when the bride and groom stood before a clergy member and took marriage vows in the presence of family and friends.

I was so engrossed in my own thoughts that I didn't realize how loud the loud music was. Sheer joy and gaiety permeated the whole neighborhood. By now, the women, elaborately dressed in colorful native garb, were doing spirited solo dancing under the canopy. They weren't entertainers because I recognized many of them as family members and friends who were present at the ceremony in the parlor.

There was lots of conversation going on in Wolof. And by then, Birdie, Suweeyah's mother, and I were the only African Americans present under the canopy, but everyone was friendly. I just sat quietly and exchanged warm, approving smiles with them as they danced flamboyantly and anything but modestly. It was delightful and enchanting, almost like a fairyland dream to me watching them dance under the canopy.

Every now and then a hot breeze wafted our way, along with that familiar aroma of cooking onions, celery, and bell pepper. I felt hunger pangs, and my stomach growled. It suddenly dawned on me that it was now late in the day, and I hadn't had anything to eat since breakfast. I comforted myself in the knowledge that, thank goodness, nobody could hear my stomach above all of the gaiety and merrymaking!

After a short while, I saw the men, all in single file in the distance, retracing their steps back toward Mamadou's house.

Out of the blue, Madame Gueye appeared and told Birdie and me to follow her. We got up, and she led us to a home up the street.

When we arrived, there was a large gathering of people. They were already assembled for the wedding reception feast. Large trays of food were being carried into the front room of that house and other houses along the street. It was apparent that relatives and friends in the neighborhood had cooperated with one another in preparing and serving the reception feast in their homes.

Madame Gueye led us into the living room of a neighbor's house. A large platter of food was set in the middle of the floor. I could see that the menu was the dish of the country—*tiebou dienne*. Of course, it was served in traditional Senegalese family style. Everyone seated themselves around the platter in the middle of the floor. In good taste, I followed their lead. We all sat down on the floor. They began serving themselves from the platter. My stomach growled again, reminding me that I was dreadfully hungry.

As hungry as I was, all of a sudden my hunger pangs left me. I wasn't hungry anymore, and so I couldn't eat.

Cautiously, I left the group seated around the platter. Trying desperately to be inconspicuous, I took a seat on a sofa nearby and watched as the others relished the feast. Of course, no one even missed me.

When they finished eating, Madame Gueye said to Birdie and me, "Come and go with me."

We followed her out of the house and walked up the street. She stopped in front of a nearby house and said, "This is the home of a friend of mine. She would like to meet you."

She led us into the house where we were introduced. We were immediately served cold soft drinks. I was again moved nearly to tears while I accepted their hospitality after such a long day for everyone.

We stayed there for just a little while and then bade them good-bye. Madame Gueye then escorted us to a community facility where many people were already assembled. I wondered why there were so many people there. Then it suddenly dawned on me that this must have been a designated place for the remainder of the wedding festivities.

As we entered, I could see familiar faces, including Monsieur Gueye, the Gueye's next-door neighbor, Mamadou's countryman who bore the same name, Mr. Badiane, and his wife. The room was full to overflowing with members of Mamadou's family and friends. Madame Gueye led Birdie and me to chairs side by side at a long table up front. Mamadou, Suweeyah, and Suweeyah's mother were already seated at the table.

Gifts were brought to the table and accolades were paid to the bride and groom. Meanwhile, I took this opportunity to ask Suweeyah again, "Are you married yet?"

This time, she replied with a broad smile, "I guess so."

Not knowing what else to say, I said, "Best wishes."

She smiled demurely and said, *"Jeredef! Jeredef!"* Not knowing what else to do, I leaned around her and said to Mamadou who was seated right beside her, "Congratulations to the both of you."

With that boyish smile on his face, he said, *"Jeredef! Jeredef!"*

Birdie and I sat there for a short time, listening to the conversations held among the guests. I smiled at them as they filed up to the table where the bride and groom were seated.

Birdie whispered to me, "I wonder what we're supposed to be doing."

I couldn't think of what else to say, so I whispered back, "I don't know. So as the old saying goes, 'when you don't know what to do, don't do anything'."

Birdie chuckled, "Then we'll just sit here."

In a few minutes, Mamadou rose from his seat and again introduced Birdie and me to the guests.

We acknowledged the introductions and sat quietly until Madame Gueye approached the table and said to us, "We will be going home now. Follow me. I am going to get a taxi to take us home."

Before we left the table, we congratulated Mamadou and Suweeyah again. They thanked us.

Like two little girls, Birdie and I followed Madame Gueye out of the building and into the street. Since it was dark by that time, I was totally disoriented and had no idea where we were in relation to Mamadou's house or in which direction we were walking. I was just walking—like a zombie or robot. My hunger pangs were back, and I felt a little weak, but I just kept walking. With Madame Gueye in the middle, a short distance ahead, two gentlemen, headed in the opposite direction, walked up to us. They said something to her in Wolof. With her answer, they changed directions, and it became apparent that they were going to escort us as we walked. Evidently they'd asked her where we were going, and when she told them she was going to get a taxicab to take us home, those gentlemen walked us to the taxi. They waited until we got in, and then they turned and walked away. Madame Gueye and Birdie talked all the way to Madame Gueye's house.

I was so hungry and exhausted, I couldn't talk.

Back to Madame Gueye's

As soon as we walked into the house, I could smell something good. Oh! My stomach growled again to remind me that by then I was ravenous. I felt dizzy and nauseous. It didn't make it any better when I acknowledged the fact that I hadn't had anything to eat since breakfast. We walked into the foyer and then into the living room where Monsieur Gueye was sitting.

I thought, *How did he get here so fast? We just saw him at the reception.* But I didn't ask.

Following Madame Gueye's lead, we slipped out of our shoes. Greeting her husband, we all sat down on the sofa, but only for a moment or two before their two house helpers began the ritual setup for serving a meal. I watched them with subdued glee as they placed that large thick, round, woven straw mat on the floor, spread a beautiful off-white damask tablecloth over it, and then set a platter of food on the tablecloth.

It was at that moment that I realized Madame Gueye had observed that I hadn't eaten at the wedding feast. In the meantime, she had somehow communicated with their house helpers and told them to prepare a meal to be served immediately upon our arrival.

We all sat down on the floor. To my delight, when I looked at the food on the platter, I feasted my eyes on calves' liver with steamed onions, fried potatoes, salad, some of her delicious homemade tomato sauce, and French bread. My heart swelled with pride.

I asked her, "Madame Gueye, how did you know that I'm so hungry?"

Demonstratively, she pointed to each one of her eyes with each index finger, smiled, and said, "I see! I see!"

That was her way of letting me know she had observed that I hadn't eaten at the feast after the wedding and that by this time I surely must have been hungry. She was so right. Secretly, I was sick from hunger.

Again I was reminded of her incomparable circumspection and spirit of loving kindness. We all began dipping into the platter of food with our fingers. Trying hard to hold back my tears, I told her, "Madame Gueye, you have made me feel like a queen! I'm enjoying this so much, and it tastes so good."

She smiled graciously. We all ate heartily. I don't know about the others, but I had to consciously keep from drooling.

When we finished and their house helpers removed the platter and setting, we all retired to the living room where Madame Gueye's husband prepared the "libation" over his charcoal stove. It was stimulating me, but I had gotten so hungry during the long day that it affected me like a sedative. I felt tranquilized, even anesthetized.

We watched a bit of television, part of which was a documentary being narrated by a person whose face was familiar to me. I asked, "Isn't that the same gentleman who does the lectures at the Slave House on the Island of Gorée?"

Almost simultaneously, they both replied, "Yes. That is Joseph Ndiaye, the principal curator of Le Maison des Esclaves."

The discourse was spoken in Wolof, but Madame Gueye told to us that the subject of the documentary was relative to a current local political issue that would not interest us. She didn't elaborate any further.

After having had such a long day and ending it by eating such a satisfying meal and libation so late, I was drowsy and felt absolutely numb. Before long, I caught myself as my head bobbed. I was nodding. I was so embarrassed. I looked around self-consciously. But I could see that everybody else was nodding, too. So I declared myself having been spent for the day and said that I was going to go to bed.

Birdie and I went to our room. We sat on the edge of our beds and recapped some of the events of the day.

Birdie reminded me of our purpose and said, "Mum Jane, we've accomplished our mission. We've witnessed Mamadou's wedding in Dakar, Senegal, West Africa—our Motherland."

As tired and sleepy as I was, I mustered enough energy to take out my journal and make a few quick notes. I closed my eyes, but my mind was still whirling.

I said to Birdie, "Oh! Tomorrow is Christmas Day. We can sleep late in the morning, because there aren't any scheduled activities that I know of. Do you know of any?"

I must have fallen asleep while saying my prayers, because I don't remember what her answer was or if she even answered me.

In fact, I don't even remember saying "Amen."

Christmas Day in Dakar

Not long after waking up and while going through the morning routine, I began thinking about the fact that I didn't know Senegalese customs on Christmas Day. Judiciously, I ventured a brief mention to Madame Gueye that it was Christmas Day, one of the most celebrated days of the year in America. Since my remark elicited no comment from anybody, I privately hailed this as the day of the birth of Christ who brought joy to our world!

Just as we sat down to our continental breakfast, one of the house helpers came in the front door with a baguette of fresh-baked French bread. I know it was freshly baked because I could smell it through the protective paper sleeve. My stomach growled and my mouth watered. I'm sure Madame Gueye heard my stomach, because she smiled at me as she broke our bread.

I'm still not sure how Madame Gueye was always able to synchronize our rising with her household routine, as if the two had been previously orchestrated. But it always worked out perfectly. Just as we started to eat, Birdie emerged from the bedroom and joined us at the table.

I heard the phone ring. Madame Gueye left the table. When she came back, she was radiant and announced, "My sister is coming to visit me today, because she's anxious to meet you."

Birdie took the words right out of my mouth when she said, "Oh, we'd love to meet your sister."

I added, "It'll be a pleasure to meet her, because I'm sure she's equally as delightful as you."

Madame Gueye smiled as she accepted my compliment.

As we left the table after breakfast, her house helpers approached the table to clear away the dishes and food. Birdie and I followed Madame Gueye into the living room and seated ourselves on the sofa.

It seemed the timing was perfect, because just then the doorbell rang. As Madame Gueye almost sprinted to the front door, she said, "Oh! That must be my sister!"

"In order for her to get here so soon, she must have been in the neighborhood," I said to Birdie before thinking, because that really wasn't any of my business.

They walked through the foyer to the living room. Madame Gueye introduced us. Her sister slipped out of her shoes and walked in. I could tell from her sister's slender build that she bordered on being petite. She was elegantly attired, and her hair looked as if it had just been coiffed. I noticed that she was carrying a rather large satchel.

As we acknowledged the introduction, I couldn't help myself when I said, "Oh, you and Madame Gueye look so much alike." As soon as I said it, I felt stupid, but I didn't catch it before it popped out.

Neither of them responded. They just smiled and sat down on the sofa across from us on the other side of the living room with their backs to the television.

As they visited with each other, Madame Gueye intermittently directed conversation to Birdie and me. Her sister didn't speak English, but I could tell that their conversation was in French. It was obvious to me that they loved each other very much and that they enjoyed each other's company, because they laughed a lot.

Madame Gueye told us that she and her sister lived quite a distance apart. I mistakenly assumed that they hadn't seen each other for a while, and when I inquired, Madame Gueye corrected me and said emphatically, "Oh no, we visit each other often."

At a lull in their conversation, her sister opened the satchel that she brought with her. She and Madame Gueye carefully spread out an enormous array of handmade authentic African garments. They made a point of telling us that her sister had made the garments. Some were one-piece, and some were two-piece. The fabrics were soft and colorful.

My eyes lingered over one garment in particular. I exclaimed, "Oh, how beautiful," as they meticulously displayed each one. But I had already made up my mind as to the garment that caught my eye. It was a two-piece blue-and-gold-patterned dress with a matching moussa. I slipped into the bedroom to try it on. It fit perfectly.

As I was I finalizing my purchase, Madame Gueye's husband came in from the garage. One of their house helpers came in with him. They were both carrying shopping bags. It was obvious that they'd been to the grocery store and the market.

In a moment, the doorbell rang again. Madame Gueye went to answer it. She returned with one of Mamadou's brothers.

At the doorway, he slipped out of his shoes and explained as he walked in, "I have come to take you, Birdie, to pick up the tailor-made garments you ordered to take back to America. It is imperative that you pick up your garments, because the tailor will close early today and also since you are leaving for The Gambia tomorrow."

Birdie responded as she got up from the sofa, "Oh yes, that's right. The tailor told me that my garments would be ready today. It's a good thing you came for me, because I had forgotten all about that," she confessed as she left to go to the bedroom to get her purse.

"No problem. No problem. It's no wonder you forgot with all that's taken place since you placed your order," he said, trying to console her. He smiled, and I could see pride in the expression on his face, knowing that he'd avoided a disappointment if she hadn't picked up her tailor-made garments.

Just then, the doorbell rang again. Madame Gueye answered and returned with a lady who explained that she had come by to meet Birdie and me, Madame Gueye's friends from America. We were introduced. I immediately realized that she didn't speak English either. But Madame Gueye was quick to pick up on this and let us know that her friend had been visiting in the neighborhood and took this opportunity to come to meet us.

At this point, it again crossed my mind that this was Christmas Day which accounted for friends and family dropping in to visit and fellowship, much as we do in America.

Seeing Birdie as she returned with her purse, speaking directly to her, Mamadou's brother advised her that they should leave immediately to get to the tailor before he closed his business for the day.

When Madame Gueye realized that Birdie would be leaving to take care of her business, she asked me if I would like to go on a sightseeing tour of Dakar while she was gone.

"Oh that would be great." I said.

Birdie and Mamadou's brother left to go into town.

Madame Gueye, her sister, their friend and I followed one another out to the garage and got into the car. Monsieur Gueye seated her friend, her sister, and me comfortably in the back seat of their Mercedes and then seated Madame Gueye in the passenger seat beside him. And off we went!

He drove through a region that was completely unfamiliar to me. At a far distance from Madame Gueye's home and in what seemed to me to be similar to a village, Monsieur Gueye stopped the car. Her friend got out.

I asked Madame Gueye, "Will you please tell your friend how happy I am to have met her and that I sincerely hope to see her again someday."

All the while, I was surmising that Madame Gueye's friend took advantage of the opportunity to get a ride home. With the motor still running, she got out and said, *"Ci Jamma!"*

I said, "Goodbye! *Ci Jamma!*"

From there, Madame Gueye's husband drove for quite a distance at what seemed like an appropriate cruising speed. We were riding through a rather sparsely populated area and bumpy roads when he gradually stopped the car at the end of a narrow road. Madame Gueye's sister said something to her which she in turn translated to mean that she was happy to have met me, because she had heard so much about Birdie and me.

I asked Madame Gueye to tell her how honored I felt that she'd made such an effort to come into town to meet us and for showing us her garments and I hoped it wouldn't be too long before we'd see each other again.

As Madame Gueye was talking to her, her sister got out of the car. She took her satchel with her as we exchanged goodbyes. The three of us rode off.

That left Madame Gueye and I in the car when Madame Gueye's husband said he would take us on a mini-tour of downtown Dakar and the surrounding areas. I told them I was sure that some sections would be familiar to me, because I'd been there before in the daytime.

It was just at dusk as we rode along. Madame Gueye translated to me from her husband's conversation that Dakar is said to be the most European city between Casablanca, North Africa, and Abidjan, West Africa.

Looking at the geology of the land, I made some deductions of my own. Dakar appeared to be on a flat elevation. At least, I didn't see any mountains or hills, even in the background.

Downtown, there were tall, modern buildings, and some of the avenues were lined with trees. Surprisingly, there were lots of people out walking around, even though it was early evening on Christmas Day. However, not many of the shops or markets were open for business at that hour. We had to stop frequently for the foot traffic, and there was lots of automobile traffic too. (The cars, trucks, and buses I saw were Peugeots, Mercedes, and Volvos. I don't recall having seen any American-made cars.)

Soon Madame Gueye announced that we were passing the Presidential Palace, that huge, mansion-style dwelling, situated far back from the street on a large expanse of land. The lawn was meticulously manicured, and there was fencing surrounding the site. Also, there was a gate along the sidewalk so that one couldn't just walk onto the grounds without admittance. Standing at attention was a tall, stately, uniformed, armed guard. Madame Gueye translated Monsieur Gueye's information that Senegal was self-governed, that the government was democratic, and that there were only black people working in government service there. She stated that most of Senegal was considered "savannah" which offered an ideal tropical vacation weather and climate. For that reason, tourism was one of its leading industries. Therefore, France still had an interest in Senegal in spite of its self-government.

They pointed out the National Assembly Building, and the Parliament House. We rode on through the financial district, passing commercial buildings that housed travel agencies, airline ticket offices, banks, restaurants, and other business establishments. We passed by the SDV Travel Agency where Birdie went to get cash on her American Express card when we were in Dakar before.

Fondly, I reflected on our last day in Dakar just a little over a year before when Birdie and I walked from the hotel to the bank in the business district to convert our CFAs back into U.S. dollars. I couldn't resist telling Monsieur and Madame Gueye about our chance meeting with the kind gentleman who helped us find our way. They laughed when I told them that we were skeptical of him at first, but when he identified himself as a friend of Mamadou's, our skepticism was put to rest.

Just then, we rounded the corner. Right before my eyes, there was a hotel. I recognized it immediately and blurted out, "Oh, there's the Sofitel Taranga Dakar Hotel, where Birdie and I stayed when we were here before."

"Yes, that is the Sofitel Taranga Dakar Hotel," Madame Gueye reassured me. "At the present time, it is one of the most popular hotels in Dakar."

I saw the street sign and recognized it as La Place de l'Indépendance.

Her husband slowed down to a crawl as he drove us through the breezeway so I could get a closer look for my nostalgia. The hotel was all lit up, and I could see guests entering and leaving and bellmen loading and unloading baggage. He drove back out onto La Place de l'Indépendance and picked up speed.

We rode on for a short distance when Madame Gueye pointed out that the section of town we were approaching was an area that was primarily residential. There were many large and handsome homes on both sides of the street. I marveled at the sight of seeing another residential area other than the one where the Gueye family and the Niang family lived.

We changed directions. I could see that we were approaching the ocean. Madame Gueye said, "We are going to the fish market. I want to shop for some fresh fish that has just been caught."

When we got there, Monsieur Gueye parked the car. We all got out and walked in the sand on the beach. Many long tables were lined up in the sand along the oceanfront, and fishermen were displaying their catches for sale. Such an enormous fish market I have never seen. Even at that hour, and it was almost dark, there were lots and lots of people browsing the display tables and buying fish. Madame Gueye made several selections and completed her purchases.

We headed back to the car. We got in and rode back to the house. From the direction in which he approached the house, this time I recognized it before we got to the driveway.

We drove into the garage. They invited me into the living room. I followed their lead by slipping out of my shoes at the doorway and seated myself comfortably on the sofa.

Madame Gueye left the room and went into the kitchen. She was gone for only a moment or two. While she was away, a thought came to my mind. When she returned and before it slipped my mind, I vowed to ask her, "What is the Wolof name of the style of garment I purchased from your sister?"

With a smile and an expression of delight that I would ask such a question, she explained very distinctly and proudly, "It is called a *dokcat*." She pronounced it like "docket."

I asked her, "Madame Gueye, will you spell that for me?"

As she spelled it, I wrote it down in my notes. I told her, "I'll be exceedingly proud to wear my *dokcat* in America since it's an authentic, handmade African garment purchased from your sister in Dakar."

"Earlier, you explained the significance of the headpiece worn by some of the women and not worn by others. I didn't make a note of your explanation, so would you be good enough to tell me again?" I asked apologetically. "What is the headpiece called, and tell me again what the cultural and traditional significance of the headpiece is?"

She promptly explained very pedagogically, "The headpiece is called a *moussa*. It is worn by married women." She further explained, "It is to be worn only by married women. However, sometimes women who are not married also wear it, as it complements their *dokcat* or *bou-bou*."

Before I finished making my notes I then asked her to tell me the difference between the *dokcat* and the *bou-bou*.

She said, "The *bou-bou* is one-piece. The *dokcat* is two-piece."

I thanked her for the information.

She commented, "You ask very interesting questions. You are like a sister to me."

I told her, "That is a compliment. I feel like a sister to you, too, Madame Gueye. Therefore, I want to learn as much about Senegal and the Wolof people as I can. I sense that I am a descendant and have felt that way ever since I met you on my Pilgrimage here last year."

Meanwhile a familiar aroma floated from the kitchen. I was embarrassed because again, my stomach growled so loudly it sounded to me like a roar. It was only then that I realized I hadn't eaten since earlier in the day. I'd been so preoccupied with so many happenings that I hadn't even thought about food.

At the same time, Mamadou's brother and Birdie came in from the tailor's shop. After slipping out of their shoes, they settled in the living room.

It was only a few moments later before the two house helpers came out and began their ritual with that large, thickly woven straw mat. They spread it in the middle of the living room floor. Over that, they spread a large damask or linen tablecloth. They returned to the kitchen and brought out a large platter and set it in the middle of the tablecloth.

Madame Gueye, her husband, Mamadou's brother, Birdie, and I all sat down on the floor in typical Senegalese style around our meal. As I took my place around the dinner platter, I was happy that the menu consisted of chicken, potatoes, steamed vegetables—no rice—Madame Gueye's delicious homemade tomato sauce, French bread, and cut-up melon and mangoes for dessert.

I couldn't resist saying, "Oh, everything looks so good!"

Immediately, Madame Gueye pointed to the chicken and smiled as she said, "Chicken is only served on special occasions, because Senegalese people eat fish and rice nearly every day."

Realizing the significance of what she told us, my eyes filled with tears. I had to consciously control them before they streamed down my cheeks, because then my nose would start to run. Again, I thanked God for answering my prayer when I left Senegal just a little over a year ago that He would spare me to be able to revisit my Motherland. And here again, He had blessed me to be seated at dinner in traditional Senegalese style in the home of some members of my African family. Furthermore, I was being served chicken because I was "special."

After dinner, we retired to the living room for conversation. While we were talking, her husband brewed tea on his charcoal stove. This time, he served us in demitasse cups.

Madame Gueye and Mamadou's brother translated information imparted by Madame Gueye's husband. As we sipped our libation, they said he expressed his pleasure that Birdie and I accepted their invitation to be their houseguests. Soon after a refill, Mamadou, Suweeyah, and her mother came in. They announced that they came to bid us farewell since Birdie and I would be leaving Dakar early the next morning in time to catch the ferry to Banjul, The Gambia.

As soon as they came in, I could see that Suweeyah was not feeling well. All of us were suggesting various remedies she could take to make her feel better. In spite of the fact that she didn't feel right, they stayed quite a while.

Mamadou, in his protective manner, lovingly and graciously stated that he wished Birdie and I a rewarding visit with our newfound family in Serrekunda. He reiterated, "Proceed on your journey with prudence and caution during your visit with your family there. I know you're excited about going to The Gambia, but be careful and cautious."

Amid the hugs and kisses, they said goodbye and wished us well.

We promised to keep in touch as we had done before. Those last few moments were bitter and sweet as Mamadou, Suweeyah, and his brother walked out the door.

Oh, how I regretted leaving my family in Dakar. But at the same time, I felt uplifted with excitement at the thought of seeing Rugie, Daphne, and Isha in Serrekunda the next day.

As soon as they left, Madame Gueye said in a very pedagogical manner, "You will be picked up here at seven o'clock tomorrow morning by your guide and his driver so you can get to the pier to catch the ferry to cross the river. You must leave that early, because the ferry leaves around one o'clock. However, that depends on the tide."

At that point and in a very gentle gesture, she handed each of us a copy of our itinerary. At the same time, she said, "I was instructed to collect eighty-eight U.S. dollars from each of you to cover the costs. I am responsible to take the money to Africa Connection Tours when I go to my office in the morning. The eighty-eight dollars covers everything—the cost of your drivers and tour guide, overland transportation from here to catch the ferry, your fare for the ferry, overland transportation from the ferry to Serrekunda, and admission to the wrestling matches in Banjul."

Hastily glancing at the itineraries, we thanked her, went to our room to get the money, came back and gave it to her.

With our itineraries now firmly in hand, Madame Gueye said, "I am going to bed now but "I will awaken you in the morning in plenty of time for you to have your breakfast before your guide arrives."

With that, we said good night and went to our room, packed up our belongings, and looked over our itineraries more carefully. I got out my portfolio and made detailed notes in my journal before I climbed into bed and went to sleep.

Off to Serrekunda, The Gambia

It seemed like I had just gone to sleep when there was a soft knock on our door. Madame Gueye cracked the door, stuck her head in and said, "It is time to get up. Your breakfast is ready."

We hurriedly got dressed and went out to the foyer where the table was already set up for us as usual. Madame Gueye joined us for our continental breakfast of orange juice, French bread, jelly, and coffee.

No sooner had we finished when there was a knock at the front door. When Madame Gueye opened it, there stood Ramou and the driver from the travel agency.

We had met Ramou the day before Mamadou's wedding day, so we all recognized one another. He was a tall, slender man who looked to be in his mid-thirties. As soon as I saw him, I remembered that he spoke fluent English, so I could get a lot of information from him while we traveled. When Mamadou introduced him to us, he said that they worked together and were good friends.

He and the driver greeted us, and Madame Gueye directed them down the hall to our room where they picked up our luggage and carried it out to the car.

Standing in the doorway, we thanked her for their hospitality and, most of all, for just being who they were and all that we meant to each other. She walked out to the car with us. We hugged and tearfully said good-bye.

In a very emotional tone of voice and looking us straight in the eyes, she said, "Thank you for being my houseguests. I am proud that you chose to stay with us."

All we could say was, "Thank you for asking us. But it was our honor and pleasure."

Ramou had opened the back door of the car and was standing there, waiting for us to get in. I got in. Birdie got in behind me, and he closed the door. The driver was already at the wheel. Ramou opened the front door and got into the passenger seat. He introduced us to our driver. The driver acknowledged the introduction in Wolof as he drove off.

Through the rear window, Birdie and I waved good-bye to dear Madame Gueye. She stood there in front of the house, smiling, as she waved us out of sight. This time, I didn't even try to hold back the tears. I could feel them streaming down my cheeks, dropping onto my T-shirt.

Again, I asked God if He would spare me to return for another reunion with my Senegalese family.

In his attempt to welcome us and put us at ease, Ramou said, "We should be arriving at the pier at Barra in plenty of time to transfer your luggage onto the ferry." He continued as he half turned in his seat to face us, "After we cross the river, we'll change cars and have a different driver. That new driver will take you all the way to Serrekunda."

"OK," we both chimed.

Again from force of habit, I watched the road and the driver as we left the city, but I soon relaxed and began to soak up all I could see and hear.

I thought it odd that there wasn't a lot of automobile traffic or foot traffic. In saying so, Ramou reminded us that it was very early in the morning.

I thought *Yes, of course. Why didn't I think about that?*

As we got further and further out of town, there was no foot traffic at all, except every now and then; eventually, there were no other cars ahead or behind us as we got onto the secondary road leading to pier.

"All this looks and feels so familiar," Birdie remarked.

"Yes, it surely does," I replied. "It's almost unbelievable that here we are back on the same road we took before on our way to catch the ferry to go to The Gambia."

In true travel-guide persona, Ramou began to orient us to the area through which we were traveling, by saying, "We'll be passing through several little villages on our way to the pier. We'll be going through Anima, Rufisque, Fatick, Saly, Kaolack, Toubecouta and on to Barra."

Hastily, I jotted down the names of the towns he named. I thought he said that Anima was the first village we'd pass through, but by the time he got it off his lips, I caught just a glimpse of the posted sign, because we'd already passed through Anima. He said that large numbers of townspeople practice Animism as a religion in that village.

Not knowing whether or not there was any relevance, I risked opening up the subject and asked him for a definition and explanation of the belief called Animism.

He gave us a cursory definition by using an example, saying, "Animism is an ancient tribal religion." He said that it espoused the belief that all earthly things had their own spiritual significance. In other words, it was the belief in the existence of spirits and that natural objects were phenomenal in that they possessed a soul. Thus, the village was named after the religion.

I asked, "Then, could that be interpreted as being sort of the opposite of atheism?"

"Perhaps," he replied in a rather noncommittal tone.

As I thought about it, there was no valid reason to pursue the subject, so I let him take the lead in opening our next dialogue.

Just then, I recognized the names of three of the other towns he named. One of them was Rufisque.

I said, "Mamadou told us that Rufisque is the village where he was born, and that his mother and some of his other family members still live there."

"Yes, that's right," Ramou replied.

"One of the other village names I remember is Kaolack. We stopped over in Kaolack on our way to the border when we were here before," I said, proud to have remembered the names.

Riding over that bumpy road brought back memories. In fact, the road felt bumpier and like it had more potholes than before. I tried to make some notes as we rode, but I had a hard time guiding my pen to stay on the line.

Turned halfway around in his seat, Ramou pensively commented, "This must be a very enriching experience for you two ladies, realizing that your ancestors were taken from their native land, never to return except through their spirits with the return of their descendants like you."

"Yes, it is. But we're very aware that many of our African ancestors who were intended to be sold in America didn't survive the ordeal and the journey," Birdie responded.

Out of the clear blue sky, Birdie asked, "Ramou, have you been to America?"

In very clear English and with a lilt in his voice, he quickly responded, "Oh yes, I have been to America numerous times. I have lots of friends in several different states in America."

I thought about what Mamadou and Madame Gueye had told us relative to the inequity by which eligibility requirements were determined for granting visas to Senegalese people who want to visit the United States.

That thought prompted me to ask him, "How do you qualify to obtain a visa when so many Senegalese people can't meet the requirements?"

With a coy smile, he was quick to answer, "I always return by the time my visa expires."

I sensed that, deliberately, he didn't elicit more dialogue on that subject, so I changed the subject and said to him. "I notice you're dressed in Western attire."

Smilingly, he responded, "Oh yes. We Senegalese people are greatly influenced by Americans. In fact, all Africans are influenced by Americans."

As I turned to the next page in my journal, my eye caught a phrase I had jotted down some time before but had forgotten to ask about. With my pen ready to record his answer, I said to him, "I know this is irrelevant, but what is cous cous in your country?"

"It is ground millet cooked and served as rice," he answered.

"OK. Now, precisely, what is millet?" I asked him.

"It is a small grain like the seed of a grass," he explained as we jostled along.

I got so drowsy from jostling up and down while riding on such a bumpy road that I had scarcely finished writing down his answer when I guess I dozed off.

A sudden jolt awakened me from my catnap. As soon as I opened my eyes, I saw what looked like a uniformed officer. He walked to the passenger side of the car. Through the window, he and Ramou exchanged a word or two.

The officer must have ordered Ramou to present some documents and to get out of the car, because Ramou reached in the glove box and took out some papers. He then turned around and said to Birdie and me, "Please give me your passports."

We handed them to him.

He and the driver got out of the car. Ramou handed the papers to the officer. They stood there for a moment or two, talking, and then the three of them leisurely walked a short distance back down the road we had just traveled.

Birdie and I were both turned in our seats so we could look out the rear window and see what on earth was going on. All the while, we were discussing what we saw. I was getting hotter and hotter. To keep sweat from dripping down onto my T-shirt, I took out my handkerchief and wiped sweat that was running from my head down to my chin. I had a flashback of the night the officer had stopped Madame Gueye when she was driving us to her home just after our arrival in Dakar.

I could see Ramou emoting with his hands as they walked and talked. When the three of them reached a shady spot under a huge tree (it looked like a baobab tree), they stood there talking for some twenty-five or thirty minutes. Partly afraid and partly angry, we mulled over what we saw. Finally we agreed on our own conclusions—that in order for us to continue on our journey, some sort of bargain was being made between the officer and Ramou.

Inside, I seethed with indignation and the letdown feeling of disrespect. Furthermore, Birdie and I had been left unattended in that hot car.

"This is most disenchanting," I groused to Birdie as if she could do something about it.

But, agreeing with me, she said, "I don't like this. I don't like this at all."

"How embarrassing it must be for Ramou and his driver to have to go through something like this. And furthermore, we've been left unattended in this hot car for all this time," I complained, repeating myself.

Finally, through the back window, we could see Ramou and our driver walking back toward the car.

As they got in, Ramou told us that a bribe had to be consummated in order for the driver to be able to proceed to our destination, the pier at Barra, to board the ferry that would take us to Banjul.

"We figured that," we both chimed, as if we'd rehearsed it.

We rode off while Ramou apologized. In a meek, modest tone of voice, he admitted, "This happens all the time, but I'm sorry it happened while you are my travelers."

In an attempt to comfort him, I said, "But we know it's not your fault."

Birdie asked, "Does this mean we'll miss the ferry?"

He turned around in his seat and said, "No, we won't miss the ferry, but we'll have to hurry getting our luggage transferred from the car to the boat. I had planned for us to have time to stop along the way, perhaps in Kaolack, for lunch and some refreshments before boarding. But depending on the situation at the time, we may or may not have time for that," he warned.

The mention of refreshments sounded really good to me and reminded me that I was hungry again because I hadn't had anything to eat or drink since breakfast at Madame Guyeye's.

We tried to lighten the mood by comparing this debacle with the unique experience we had the previous year while traveling overland from Dakar across the dividing line of the two countries on our way to The Gambia where we met our friends Rugie, Daphne, and Isha last year. But I wasn't sure that it did anything to brighten the mood.

I just couldn't resist boasting about how painstakingly we had confirmed travel plans faxed to us through Mr. Badiane's travel agency so that we could retrace our route and relive the experience of the overland journey from Senegal to The Gambia to visit our family in Serrekunda.

As we jostled along, I said to Birdie, "It seems to me that we're either going faster than before we were stopped, or there are more potholes in the road."

She agreed, saying, "It's probably a combination of both. But at least we're on our way."

There wasn't much conversation during the rest of the journey. However, I was still seething with rage. I felt justified at being resentful of the inconvenience and resolved then and there to document my resentment in a letter to Mr. Badiane when I returned to Hayward. The more I thought about it, the more I was offended by the lack of respect paid to us as African descendants, having returned to our Motherland for such a prestigious event, Mamadou's wedding. In the corner of my mind, I did reserve some contrition that Ramou and his driver also had to go through such humiliation and succumb to sleaze and corruption in order to do their job.

While I was mulling things over in my mind, I realized that we had come to a rather abrupt stop. Surveying the land, I realized that I had fumed us into the Pier of Barra.

The ferry was in port. As soon as the car stopped, Ramou and the driver got out and began hurriedly transferring our luggage from the car to the ferry. While Birdie and I were standing nearby, just watching them do their job, I noticed a group of young boys standing alongside a chain-link fence. Slowly, one of the boys began walking toward us.

Birdie recognized the boy, and it was obvious that the boy recognized her, because almost simultaneously as he walked directly up to her with a great big smile on his face, he called out to her, "Ms Birdie! Ms Birdie! Do you remember me? Do you remember me? I'm Oriano!"

Birdie responded, but began asking him questions all in one breath.

"Yes, I remember you, Oriano! You're the young man who asked me to send him some books. I sent some books to you. Did you receive them? And did you read them?"

"Yes, I received them, Ms Birdie, and I read them," he replied, as he reached out to shake her hand. He still had that great big smile on his face which could only be interpreted as pure joy, surprise, amazement, and shock. Just think that after all the time that had elapsed, this young man was standing at a point where we would meet again.

Birdie continued, "Well, I'm glad you got the books, because I wondered if you received them.

Do you remember what the books were about?" she quizzed him again all in one breath.

"Yes, I remember. The books were biographies about Martin Luther King and a biography on Malcolm X. And I thank you, Ms Birdie!"

"Remember, I told you to share the books with your family and friends after you read them. Did you do that?"

"Yes! Yes, I did, Ms Birdie!" he replied.

"You told me you would write to me to let me know that you got the books and if you liked them, but I didn't hear from you. Why didn't you write to me?" she queried.

With a sincere look of apology, he answered, "Ms Birdie, I did not write to you because I did not have a stamp, and I did not have any money to buy a stamp."

Just then, Ramou called to her to board the ferry, but she was able to have a few last words with Oriano, saying, "Well, that's all right. I guess it was meant to be that you and I would meet on this very special day here at the pier at Barra. The amazing thing is that you would be here at this very moment when I'm getting ready to board the ferry to Banjul."

She called him by his name and said, "It's just wonderful meeting you here and having these few moments to talk to you, but I must go now. Take good care of yourself, and I do hope we can meet again someday."

She walked over to where Ramou and I were standing, waiting for her to join us to board the ferry. As she waved good-bye to Oriano, it saddened me to see the look on his face.

Anxious to continue on our journey, I wondered where our driver was, but soon remembered that our guide told us we'd change cars after the crossing, so it made perfectly good sense that our driver wouldn't be making the ferry trip into Banjul with us. I don't know when he disappeared. I regretted that I didn't have a chance to thank him and say good-bye.

Along with us, there were lots and lots of passengers getting on the ferry. Most of them stayed on the first level, but Ramou led us up those steep steps to the upper level. Like a recording in my head, I could hear myself asking our former guide on our Pilgrimage why he always took us to the upper deck of the ferry and positioned us by the lifesavers. No less overpowering was his reply, and I could hear it as clearly as the day he said it, "*Because I don't know how to swim.*"

When we got up there, I looked around as Ramou lead us to an area on the shady side of the boat. That upper level was almost full, but more passengers filled in wherever there was standing room. There were no more seats available, so we stood together.

With a sudden jolt, the motor revved up in that familiar deafening roar. We slowly began our voyage across the Gambian River. As usual, we had to shout over the roar of the engine in order to hear one another in conversation.

I looked over the railing onto the lower level. All I could see from my vantage was what looked like a huge compartment of sand below us.

I shouted to Ramou, "What a unique idea to have a sandbox for children to play in during the trip."

He looked down over the railing to see what I was talking about. He smilingly looked back at me and said, "That's not a sandbox. That's the bed of a truck loaded with sand. That truck will deliver the sand to some location in The Gambia, probably to a construction site in Banjul."

I was literally stunned. To digest what he'd told me was frightening. Just to acknowledge the possible consequence of a truck that size with a trailer loaded with sand—along with all of us passengers, freight, baggage, cargo, and who knows what else had been loaded onto that ferry—was terrifying. Only one thought permeated my mind at that point, and that was whether or not the ferry could navigate the waters with all that weight.

I tried to comfort myself in the fact that they did this all the time. The only way I could allay my fear was to completely dismiss the thought from my mind, blank it out, and just ride. I looked around and became engrossed in lighter thoughts. I began admiring the well-dressed African women. It looked as if all of them were wearing makeup—lipstick, eyebrow pencil, and mascara. They were dressed in their brightly colored *dokcats, bou-bous, and moussas*. I felt better educated for having asked Madame Gueye for the proper names of women's apparel.

By that time, the ferry had worked up enough steam so that the motor wasn't quite so loud. However, it was still very noisy.

I guess Ramou could sense that I had recovered from shock. He reopened conversation about his having been to America several times by shouting, "You know, it's wonderful to have been assigned as your guide for this journey. I've been to America many times, so I know many African Americans in several states. But I have a very special lady friend in America. She has talked of marriage, but I haven't made up my mind to do that yet."

"I'm not surprised that you've had proposals for marriage," I shouted back, "because you appear to be a very fine young man and at the age to be considering marriage and a family."

I know he heard me, but he didn't reply. He just smiled.

Already, I could feel the captain reducing his speed, because we were pulling into port for debarkation in Banjul. Having taken the same ferry trip several times before, crossing the river didn't seem to take as long as it had the first time. My thoughts and fears returned, but I breathed a sigh of relief as we landed. I just wanted to get off of that boat as soon as I could.

A car and a new driver were waiting for us at the port. I didn't need to understand what the driver and Ramou were saying as they greeted each other, because their expressions and gestures left no doubt that they had done business together before. The driver transferred our luggage to the car.

Ramou introduced us to him, pointing out that we were from America—Birdie from Ohio, and I, her mother-in-law, from California. He acknowledged the introduction with a broad smile and warm handshake. We all got in the car and took off for Serrekunda, The Gambia.

Arrival at the Badala Park Hotel

It was midafternoon when we arrived. We went directly to the Badala Park Hotel registration desk to check in. Birdie and I had stayed before. I had another mental and emotional flashback. We presented our documents, and the registration process went smoothly, without a hitch. We thanked Ramou and said good-bye to him.

As they processed our reservation, I couldn't resist reminding Birdie, "Remember what happened when we were here before?"

"Yes, how well I remember that they didn't have a reservation for us," she recalled.

"But when I produced that letter from our travel agency to the Gambian consulate, we were assigned to one room and then moved to another room with what they called 'air conditioning'. I've often wondered what would have happened if I hadn't brought along that letter. Do you suppose the Gambian consulate would have known we were in their country on a visa?"

"You know, we never did get an explanation as to why they didn't have a room reservation for us," she mused.

"That's right," I agreed.

By that time, there was an attendant at our sides to assist us with our luggage. We followed him to our room. This time, our room was street level, way in the back of the compound. As a matter of fact, we had to walk down a long, winding walkway and then around the corner to get to our room.

After we checked everything out, we situated our baggage so we could relax into the ambience and atmosphere of our surroundings. It was a nice room, modestly furnished with twin beds and a pullout sofa bed. But it didn't have a phone.

We shared some of the refreshments we'd brought along, and then after a few minutes, almost with bated breath, Birdie said, "Jane, let's go to the office and call the girls. They're expecting to hear from us this afternoon."

"OK, let's go! I can't wait to see Isha's face when she gets her doll. And then, what will the girls do when we give them all of their cosmetics and toiletries? Let's go now," I urged.

Rugie and Daphne were devoted sisters whom we met quite by chance when we were in Serrekunda the year before. They were refugees who fled to The Gambia during the height of terrorism and violence which had broken out in their native land, Sierra Leone.

Rugie was married and had a daughter. She appeared to me to be more ethnic and the least westernized of the two sisters. Daphne was unmarried, but the two obviously had a very close relationship.

As a result of our chance meeting, we established a kinship and have stayed in close touch with one another, even to this day. Our sole purpose for traveling to The Gambia on this occasion was to reunite with them.

I took Isha's doll from my luggage. Birdie took the girls' bag of toiletries and cosmetics from her luggage. We grabbed our purses. Birdie picked up our litter bag.

"Along the way, I'll drop our litter bag in that receptacle I saw right there alongside the walkway leading to the hotel lobby," she told me.

She locked up our room, and we headed for the lobby.

When we got there, Birdie placed the call. She talked for a moment and then she handed the phone to me. Surely enough, they told me they were waiting for a call from us and said they'd be at the hotel in about five minutes. Rugie said that her husband was going to drop them off on his way to take care of some business downtown.

Reuniting with Our Family in Serrekunda

It seemed like it was only in the twinkling of an eye when the girls and Isha arrived in a pickup truck driven by an African gentleman. They literally hopped out of that truck. We rushed out to greet them. We all hugged and embraced one another. Rugie introduced the gentleman to us as her husband. I observed that he seemed a little uneasy, probably because he didn't speak English. Immediately, he said good-bye. Rugie assured us that we'd see him again later that day.

As he left us standing there, I noticed that he, too, had distinctive African male characteristics. He was tall, slender, and regal-looking. He took long strides as he walked back to the pickup. He waved to us as he drove off.

We all walked around to the patio by the swimming pool. Of course, Isha was walking steadily for her age. She was an infant and not walking yet when we'd first met her.

We settled in at a table by the pool. Rugie seated Isha in a chair beside her. We ordered refreshments as we explored one another's activities since we were last together.

Rugie was medium height, slender and bordering on being petite. She looked to be in her mid-to-late twenties. She was dressed in an ethnic, subdued *dokcat* and sandals.

Daphne was about Rugie's height—maybe a little taller. She looked to be a bit younger than her sister. She was wearing lipstick, blush, mascara, and eyebrow pencil, all meticulously applied. She was dressed in Western-style attire—tight-fitting pants, a T-shirt, and sandals.

Isha, whom Birdie and I affectionately named "Our African Queen Baby," was wearing a long bright-colored print dress and sneakers. Small, multicolored beads had been braided through her plaits. One of her plaits fell casually down over the center of her forehead. She was wearing round-shaped sunglasses with dark lenses. I remembered that the pupils of her eyes appear to be coal black, protruding from her snow white eyeballs. She had a shiny oval-shaped face, and her lips were pursed, ready to break open with a smile.

I took Isha's doll from the dollmaker's plastic bag and presented the doll to her, saying, "Isha, I brought this doll to you from America. It was made by a friend of mine who is a doll maker."

Her eyes were fixed on mine as she reached out her arms and took the doll. She took a good long look at it. She put her arms around it and held it in a full embrace. Then she looked back at me with what felt like an electrifying stare. It was almost mesmerizing.

Isha Embracing Her American-made Doll

Her mother asked her, "Isha, what do you say to Sister Jane? She has brought you a present all the way from America."

Isha took a quick glance at her mother, looked down at her doll, and then looked back at me and said, "Thank you. Thank you."

I was moved and had to fight back the tears. She was hugging that doll with both arms as the server brought our refreshments.

"Oh, how good it is to see all of you, and you look so good," we exclaimed. They returned the compliments.

"Tell us about the wedding," they asked between sips of their drinks.

"Oh, it was very different from what we expected and what we're accustomed to in America," I answered.

"You'll have to read about it in Mum Jane's book, because she's going to write all about this trip," Birdie divulged, revealing my secret.

We told them about our experience at the border leaving Senegal and entering The Gambia. They didn't appear to be surprised, and when we vented on them, they explained that they'd heard about similar incidents happening with foreign travelers and even with some of the natives.

"That makes me all the more determined to document my thoughts on paper to Mr. Badiane when I get back home," I vowed.

They said they regretted that it had happened to us. But somehow I got the feeling that they weren't convinced that anything would be done about it.

By this time, we had finished our refreshments, and the girls asked us to walk with them to their home.

Rugie said, "It is not very far. In fact, it is just a little ways up the road."

"Oh, that would be wonderful! It was on that same road that we met you. Remember?" Birdie responded almost before Rugie got the words out of her mouth.

"We have prepared a meal for you and would be happy for you to spend the rest of the day with us," Daphne added.

Birdie picked up the bag of cosmetics and toiletries. We all left the pool area and slowly followed them out onto the road leading to their home. All the while, Isha was hugging her doll.

When we arrived and went inside, Birdie gave the bag to Rugie and Daphne. As they opened the bag, their eyes opened almost equally as wide as the bag. They sat down on the floor and put the bag down between them and began going through the contents like it was a treasure chest of jewels. They were like two little girls on Christmas morning opening surprise packages of presents. They thanked Birdie profusely and told her how much they liked what she had brought to them and how useful the items were, because some of the items weren't available to them in Serrekunda. Birdie and I looked at each other with smiles of confirmation that we had brought joy to all of these new family members.

I noticed that all the while, Isha was still hugging her doll.

They invited us into the other rooms of the house. I observed that the house was immaculately clean. It was modestly furnished, and I felt comfortable and relaxed. They took us outside. Likewise, the backyard area was conducive to comfort and relaxation. However, there were no trees for shade, and it was a bright, sunshiny day, so it was very hot out there for me.

Leisurely, we walked back inside and sat down to the meal they had prepared for us. It was chicken, rice, and vegetables. It was most welcome, because we hadn't eaten since breakfast at Madame Gueye's, and by now it was late in the afternoon. We lingered at the table, talking, for quite a while.

During dinner, Daphne rather delicately asked, "Would you let us take you to a village to meet a friend?"

Rugie added, "We met her in Kotu after we took up residence in The Gambia."

Of course we accepted the invitation with excitement and anticipation.

"Birdie, don't forget that we have an appointment to be picked up to go to the wrestling matches," I reminded her.

Immediately, Daphne excitedly interjected, "OK, we'll get you back in time for that, but we want to take you to the village so our friend can meet you."

"We have told her all about you, and she is looking forward to our bringing you out there," Rugie added.

It was almost dark when Rugie's husband came in. Rugie translated to us that he apologized for being away so long but explained that he had been delayed in carrying out some details pertaining to their business matters. However, he told us that whenever we were ready to go back to the hotel, he would be happy to take us.

While he ate his dinner, we all sat with him and talked about our special time of fellowship with Mamadou's family and Madame Gueye's family. Rugie proudly showed him Isha's doll and the bag of toiletries and cosmetics we'd brought them from America.

At what seemed like the opportune moment, Rugie told her husband that we had accepted their invitation and were excited about going to the village to meet their friend.

When he finished eating his dinner, we all walked out of the house together. I noticed that Isha was still affectionately clutching her doll.

Rugie's husband was driving the same pickup truck. Rugie and Daphne apologized for not having a sedan. A picture flashed through my mind of how all of us were going to get to that village the next day.

We all got into the truck. Rugie's husband drove us back to the Badala Park Hotel, which was just a short distance. While we were standing outside, Rugie's husband told us to be ready to go at eight o'clock in the morning. We assured them we'd be on time, ready, and waiting for them. We bade them goodnight with hugs.

Birdie and I walked back to our room, recapping the events of the day.

Counting on her fingers, she said, "Just think, Mum Jane, we were in Dakar, Senegal, this morning. We spent a good part of the day traveling and now we're in Serrekunda, The Gambia, another country in Africa. What an adventuresome day."

Quickly, I added, "And tomorrow we're going to a village."

While Birdie was showering, I picked up my journal and made some detailed notes.

As soon as she got out of the shower, she crawled into her bed and said goodnight.

While showering, I was in joyful self-indulgence that Isha had instantaneously bonded with her doll. Also, I took pleasure in recapturing the girls' facial expressions and excitement as proof that they were genuinely delighted with their assortment of toiletries and cosmetics.

I set the alarm on my travel clock for seven o'clock. Wearily, I crawled into my bed.

Off to Brufut Marimma Village

When the alarm went off, I could hear the eerie chant in the distance—a tranquil reminder that I was still in my Motherland.

We promptly got up and dressed in time to have some breakfast before our friends came to pick us up. The breakfast was set up buffet style with a wide selection of juices, mangoes, bananas, grapes, papayas, oranges, cheeses, boiled eggs, French bread, and coffee. I noticed the absence of breakfast meat. I pacified myself that the eggs would provide the protein for my day.

Having Breakfast in the Badala Hotel Dining Room

After making our selections, we seated ourselves at a table situated in what seemed to me like the same table where we sat before.

I said to Birdie, "Remember, one morning when we were here on our Pilgrimage, when we came down for breakfast, the dining room was closed?"

"Yeah, and I especially remember that the owner just happened to walk through about that time and ordered the staff to serve us breakfast anyhow," she recalled.

"And remember that skinny, hungry cat I fed with nibbles from my breakfast plate?"

She said, "Yes, I remember how poised that cat was as it sat there waiting for you to drop another goodie until apparently it had enough, and then it got up and walked away. That cat was hungry, Jane."

We finished our breakfast in plenty of time, so we meandered into the hotel gift shop to browse until our friends came to pick us up. We bought some post cards, trinkets, and memorabilia. After a few moments, our friends arrived to pick us up to the village.

It was obvious that all prearrangements were well-thought out. With no further ado, Isha's father situated her in the passenger seat. Birdie and I followed Rugie and Daphne's lead and climbed into the bed of the pickup truck. As I situated myself on one of the benches along the railing on one side, I could see beverages, snacks, and some other provisions in small boxes and bags.

Just as we rode off, Rugie told us we'd be stopping at a market to pick up something. From the main boulevard, we rode into the parking lot of a supermarket. I remembered it, because Birdie and I picked up some items in that same market when we were there before. We stayed in the truck while Rugie's husband went inside. He came back after just a couple of minutes. He was carrying a small shopping bag. Somehow, I thought he was carrying a bag of ice. He got back in the truck, and we rode off.

As soon as we were rolling again, Rugie asked us if we would mind if they took a few minutes and stopped off to prepare a document at a place nearby called Gamtel where she could do some word processing.

When we got there, Rugie, Daphne, Birdie and I got out. Isha and her father stayed in the truck. I took a good look around at the crude edifice of the establishment. It reminded me of our state-of-the-art facilities in California where customers rent time on computers. After we got inside, I discovered that they needed help on the computer with processing some kind of document. They pointed out the help they needed. Of course, my input was nil because at that time, I was still getting a thrill from having finally acquired enough skill to successfully turn my computer off and on.

Birdie volunteered to help them. In fact, she took charge of it, did it, and in just a few minutes, we were out of Gamtel.

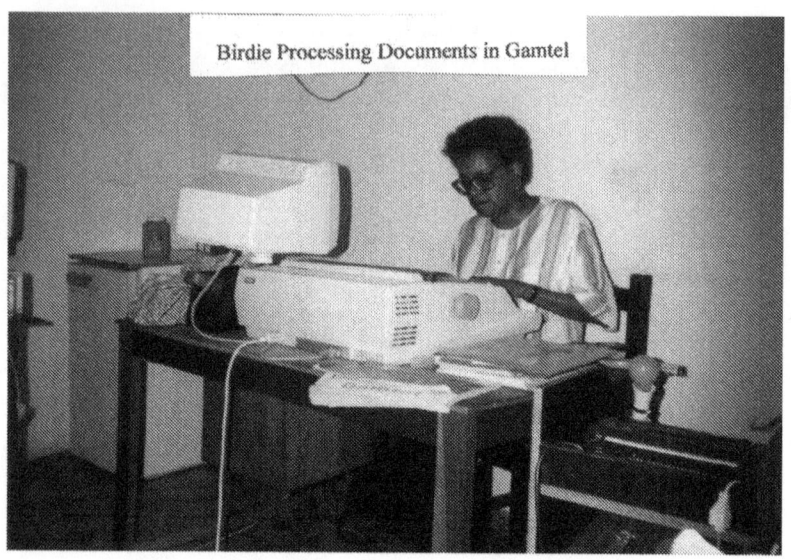

Birdie Processing Documents in Gamtel

They thanked her profusely and marveled at her skill and expertise in being able to process their documents with so little effort.

With that out of the way, we all got back on the truck and took off again.

"Now we're on our way to Brufut Marimma Village," Rugie proudly announced.

"It's not such a long way, but while we're riding, we can have some beverages and snacks," Daphne offered as she ostentatiously took out four crystal stemware goblets and handed one to each of us. She began pouring.

Yes, she poured our refreshments in crystal stemware goblets, serving me first, as the eldest, then Birdie, and then some for Rugie and herself last.

We all giggled at one another, saying, "Here we are riding along in the back of a pickup truck in the hot sun in The Gambia, West Africa, drinking from crystal stemware goblets."

As we sipped, we helped ourselves to the snacks they'd brought along.

For just a short distance, we rode on a paved four-lane highway. Then we turned off onto a bumpy two-lane road until that road narrowed to what I can only describe as a trail.

I held my breath as we entered that trail and said to Birdie, "I wonder what he'll do if another car or truck approaches from the opposite direction."

"I guess one of them will have to back up and let the other one pass. Thank goodness there isn't any traffic, because there's obviously only one-way in and one-way out," she reasoned.

To erase the thought from my mind, I asked for a refill in my goblet. Daphne obliged. I sipped on my beverage, pigged out on the snacks, and sat quietly. The truck rocked gently from side to side as we jostled into and out of potholes on the trail. There was no shoulder on the trail, so Rugie's husband had to follow tire tracks that had been hollowed out over time.

The area was remote and overgrown with dry vegetation. On both sides of the trail were scattered clumps of trees and spiny-looking shrubs. On the right side of the trail were tall, spindly, leafy trees. A slight hot wind blew the tree branches our way. The leaves on the branches slapped us in the face as we rode along, so we did what we saw Rugie and Daphne do. We whacked and slapped at the branches to keep the leaves from hitting us in the face. It seemed like we were traveling no more than about five miles an hour. It was a sensible speed, though, because it was obvious that this was not really a road, just a trail.

Jostling along, sipping our refreshments and swatting at the leaves on the overhanging branches, the truck stopped suddenly. We had just passed a young woman and two little children walking along beside her. They were walking on the side of the trail in the direction we were traveling. The woman and the two little children were all carrying plastic bags. The bags looked like they were heavy.

In a native tongue, Rugie and Daphne said something to the lady. I assumed they asked her if she wanted a ride, because the lady eagerly and willingly hopped onto the back of the truck with us. Rugie jumped out and helped the two little children into the cab of the truck beside Isha.

After she got back with us, we rode for a little ways further. All the while, we were brushing back those branches. Rugie, Daphne, and the lady held a conversation until Rugie knocked on the back window of the truck. That was a signal for her husband to stop.

As soon as he stopped, the lady jumped off the back and went around to the passenger side and got the two little children. They stood there until the truck started rolling again. We waved goodbye to them, and until they were out of sight, we could see them standing there, smiling and waving back at us.

There was no sign of dwellings or buildings within my sight, so apparently their destination was somewhere beyond that trail, back behind those dry shrubs, spiny bushes, and tall trees swaying in the wind.

Everyone was silent as we waved them out of sight until Birdie asked, "Is that lady a friend of yours?"

Daphne was quick to reply, "Oh no. We do not know her."

Rugie interrupted and added, "But my husband could see that she might want a ride, and so he stopped."

Birdie commended them, saying, "What a magnificent act of kindness. You see, in our country, even though we'd like to extend such kindnesses, we couldn't dare do that for fear of being exploited, assaulted, or even murdered."

"Is that right?" they both asked with looks of surprise on their faces. Each in her own words made it clear to us that they don't have that kind of fear.

Rugie said, "When we see people who need help, if we can help them, we do it."

"That is just the way we are." Daphne added.

"That's just wonderful," Birdie said.

All the while we were rocking and rolling along, Daphe refilled all of our goblets. As we came to a slight clearing on the trail, I could feel the truck was slowing down to a crawl.

I leaned over to look to the front of the truck. There stood a lady, several little children, and three gentlemen. They were smiling and waving at us. It was clear to me then that this was not a surprise visit; they were expecting us and we had arrived.

Hurriedly, we finished our drinks. The truck rocked to a complete stop, and we all got out. Immediately, Rugie's husband went around to the back of the truck. By the time he got there, he was joined by two of the gentlemen. They began unloading the truck and taking the provisions into the house.

Standing together in front of the house, Rugie and Daphne affectionately took Birdie and me by our hands and began making introductions. All at the same time, I was looking around. When I didn't see any other houses nearby, I had to remind myself that we were in the "bush." We were in Brufut Marimma Village.

Their friend led us into her house and motioned for us to be seated. There wasn't enough seating for all of us, so I just stood. At that very moment, from both sides of the entrance to the house, neighbors were bringing chairs—enough chairs for all of us.

We sat in that room for a few minutes while Daphne and Rugie told her friends of our relationship, including that I was from California and that Birdie was from Ohio. Mystification and bewilderment radiated from the villagers' facial expressions and in their eyes as they listened to what they were being told. The little children were standing in front with their eyes fixed on us. They were literally staring at us out of those beautiful black pupils surrounded by the clear white of their eyeballs. I was enchanted with their almost hypnotic stares. I wondered if they had ever seen or heard of any African Americans. They, too, looked at us as if they were in awe of what they were seeing and hearing—these people Daphne and Rugie called their friends from America. Frankly, I felt humble, but center stage.

Soon the lady of the house motioned for Birdie and me to follow her. She led us out the back door and into the yard. I walked over to a bench in the shade under a large, spreading mahogany tree. The lady went back inside. Rugie and Daphne followed.

In the meantime, the youngsters served us cold beverages. One by one, they all came back outside. They were carrying large serving bowls of food, plates, and flatware. A large platter of food was set before us on a long table set up just beyond the back door. We were invited to the table to serve ourselves.

While we were gathered at the table, Daphne and Rugie proudly announced, "We fixed this meal at home for you and brought it with us. It is the dish of our country, Sierra Leone. It is fundi, millet, and sauce."

It flashed through my mind that Rugie and Daphne had told us that they were refugees from Sierra Leone and that during a coup d'état in their country, they had managed to flee Sierra Leone and take refuge in The Gambia.

But before they'd picked up Birdie and me at the Badala Park Hotel, they had prepared and packed this meal. I marveled at their resourcefulness for those provisions so neatly packed in the back of the truck.

We expressed our appreciation for the honor being paid to us on that occasion. We asked Rugie and Daphne to compliment and thank their friend, our hostess, for her gracious hospitality. She was standing next to them. And all the while she, too, had a fixed, piercing stare back and forth from Birdie to me. While I filled my plate, Rugie explained that some of the people present were "originals" who lived in the vicinity of their friend's house. I didn't quite understand the significance of that statement. Nevertheless, I made a mental note to later record what she said.

Both Daphne and Rugie continued to share small talk while we were serving ourselves. The others were standing around the table and on the periphery. They, too, were staring at us, these two women Daphne and Rugie called their African American sisters. As an aside, Rugie reminded us that they had told us that here we were, guests in the home of their friend whom they met in Kotu.

When I finished filling my plate, I sauntered over and sat down on a bench in the shade under a huge mahogany tree. I opened my portfolio and made a couple of quick notes in my journal.

My Unexpected Interview with the Village Chief

While Rugie was still talking and I was making notes, a young man leisurely walked in my direction. He was carrying a hefty plate of food. To my utter surprise, he smiled and came over and sat down right beside me on the bench. He appeared genial and open. So out of sheer courtesy, but with reticence, I ventured to casually introduce myself, not expecting him to understand me. To my amazement, he acknowledged the introduction in plain English.

I was momentarily speechless with astonishment, but not so much so that I didn't muster the courage to open up a dialogue. Depending on how that went, I'd ask him some questions.

So to break the ice, I told him of my extraordinary experience the year before in the village of Juffure where I'd had a short visit with the village chief, Binta Kinte. She spoke no English, but our travel guide very expertly translated that she was the widow of the griot whose oral history provided Alex Haley with the vital African segment of his genealogy.

Nodding his head, he told me, "Oh! I have visited that village many times."

He went on to tell me that there was a woman chief in a nearby village called Basse. (I considered that information at that point in our dialogue to be relevant and concluded that most village chiefs were males.)

I asked him to spell the name for me. I wrote it as he spelled it.

"Do you live here in this village?" I asked.

"Yes, I live here in this village," he replied. His English diction was eloquent, with just a slight discernible accent. (It sounded British.)

My next question was, "Does this village have a chief?"

With a broad smile and look of surprise, he was quick to answer. He turned to me and said, "Yes, there is a village chief of Brufut Marimma. I am the village chief."

I must admit I was even more stunned to learn this than I had been when he acknowledged my introduction in English. So to seize this once-in-a-lifetime opportunity, I couldn't resist asking him his name.

Apparently, he noticed that I was making notes, because he eagerly asked for my pen. I handed my pen and notebook to him. He wrote the following:

When he returned my pen and journal, I looked down at his notations.

I asked, "Kindly assist me with the pronunciation of your name and the name of your village."

He eagerly smiled and responded.

I made several valiant attempts to enunciate. I don't know why, but I was greatly impressed by the eloquence with which he spoke, and I concluded that this man was very well educated. It was apparent to me that he welcomed my interest and if I pursued a dialogue, he would subsequently volunteer facts and historical background information.

Turning toward him so I could look into his eyes, I confessed, "I'm honored to meet you, sir, and I'd consider it a privilege if you'd talk with me."

With no prompting, he told me that The Gambia was a developing country in western Africa. He reminded me that the capital was Banjul. He said that the official language was English.

He told me that in 1960, there had been a rebellion in The Gambia. At that time, the country had won its independence from England. He said that back then, the people in the "bush" were relatively uninformed about political issues. As a result, "leaders," as they were called, were able to convince the villagers of their causes. And so, they followed the leaders' passions and convictions.

He went on to say that traditionally, the majority of the inhabitants of The Gambia practice the Muslim religion. They lived in farming villages, and most of the village population was engaged in agriculture, cultivating rice, millet, and peanuts. They raised cattle, sheep, and goats for local consumption.

He said, "The primary ethnic population in this village belongs to the Jula tribe, but some of the people who settled here during the rebellion were refugees from the Casamance in Senegal."

It was then that I connected his statement to what Rugie had told us earlier—that some of the visitors who had come to meet us were "originals," as she called them.

As I made notes, I was humbled by the realization that here and now, I had the rare honor of visiting another village in West Africa. Even more humbling was the fact that quite by coincidence, here I was talking to the Chief of the village of Brufut Marimma, Kombo North Western Division, The Gambia, West Africa.

Enthused beyond my wildest expectations, the conversation led me to ask him if he had duties and responsibilities or if his position as village chief was merely perfunctory.

Emphatically, he answered, "Oh yes, I have many duties and responsibilities to perform. And no, my position is not merely perfunctory."

I was further impressed by the fact that he answered my questions in the same sequence in which I asked them. I just couldn't abstain from asking him if he would share with me what some of his duties were as village chief.

Appearing eager to respond, and almost impetuously, he said, "To name a few, I am held responsible for administrating the affairs of the village. I am expected to be able to help resolve domestic problems, and I am frequently asked to assist in settling disputes between villagers."

He told me that as village chief, he must hold village meetings on a regular basis and he was frequently sought after for defining needs and innovating ways to develop projects that will help to meet those needs in order to improve the quality of life in his village.

He went on to say, "Land values in Brufut Marimma village are set by elders in the village, but as chief, I am responsible for collecting annual taxes on the land and sending those taxes to the central government."

With an air of pride, he said, "In general, as the village chief, I am responsible for establishing and maintaining a community atmosphere of togetherness for the tranquility of life in my village."

Forcing the issue, I queried, "Aren't all of those duties an overwhelming responsibility?"

"Yes." he articulated very emphatically. "The position is much more than just a title. It is a grave undertaking of responsibility and accountability."

"How did you become the village chief?" I asked.

Almost before I finished my question, he replied, "A village chief emerges as a leader from among founders of a village or longtime family members living in the village."

I asked him if he had projected long-range plans on his drawing board.

He was quick to reply by saying, "Yes. Two of my long-range plans are to establish a market for the shopping convenience of villagers and to construct a well for their safety in case of fire."

While he was talking, our hostess came over and sat on the other side of me. We smiled at each other as I acknowledged her presence. But since she didn't speak English, I continued my conversation with the village chief. Off and on, I glanced over at her. With an approving look on her face, she appeared to be listening intently to what her village chief was telling me. Maybe it was my optimism and hopefulness, but that's how I read her facial expression.

When he named his long-range plans for his village, I reflected on the lady and two little children we had picked up on our way out there. I told him of the scenario, noting that they must have walked a long way to shop, and how much more convenient it would have been if they had been able to shop in a local market. He agreed that a market in his village would be a boon in many ways.

Relative to his other long-range plan, I looked around at the environs and wondered just what would happen if a fire broke out. How would it be contained? But I didn't ask him, because that was a morbid thought.

Suddenly from around the side of the house, I noticed a skinny dog came over and lay down on the ground next to our hostess. I wanted to pet the dog but thought better of it.

Gradually, everyone had finished eating, and the food was taken back into the house. Shortly thereafter, a small boy came out of the back door. He was carrying a handful of stuff. He threw it down on the ground in front of the dog. The stuff he threw down was scraps of food. I glanced down at it. I saw chicken bones in it. The dog stood up and ate heartily, cracking those chicken bones and chewing everything up with no apparent difficulty. I winced at the sight and sound. I wondered how far they'd have to travel to the nearest veterinarian if that dog had gotten one of the splintered chicken bones caught in his throat or intestines.

I thought about Combo, our dog, and all the dogs we ever had before Combo. Chicken bones were strictly forbidden for all of them. They could have only ham bones or beef bones—no chicken, fish, or turkey bones. But when that dog finished chewing up everything, including those chicken bones, he went over to a pot of water under the mahogany tree. Swarms of flies were buzzing around his water pot, but the dog took a big drink of water, made a circle and lay down in the shade of the mahogany tree with the rest of us. He looked around at us as if he were enjoying the fellowship with people as much as Birdie and I, the children, and adults were enjoying the fellowship with one another.

The sun had gone down a bit, and it was a little cooler. I could see that Rugie made the first move to indicate that it was time to go. The men began loading the truck. I wanted so much to stay a while longer. But I realized that certainly there wouldn't be any lights on that trail we had to travel back to Serrekunda, so it made good sense that we should be headed back before dusk.

I closed my portfolio, thanked the village chief and said, "I'm honored to have had this unexpected experience of meeting and talking with you. I sincerely wish I could talk longer, but we have engaged the services of a guide to pick us up at the Badala Park Hotel to take us to the wrestling match. We've heard so much about it as the one of your country's favorite sports. I wish you personal well-being, all good wishes, and continued success with the administration of your duties as the chief of Brufut Marimma village. Thank you again for sharing this time with us."

He smiled at me, nodded his head, and said, "Enjoy the sporting event and the rest of your trip to The Gambia."

As we walked around the house to the truck, we thanked our hostess and her family, friends, and neighbors, climbed back into the back of the pickup truck and bade all of them farewell.

We headed back in the opposite direction. As I looked down that road, it looked even more like a trail than before. We rocked and rolled and bounced along. Thankfully, the tree branches we fought going into the village were on the other side of the trail on our way back to town, so we didn't have to contend with the leaves slapping us in the face.

As usual, the ride back to Serrekunda from the village didn't seem as long as it had seemed going into the village. So before I knew it, we were back on the main boulevard. There, I recognized many local landmarks along the route that led us back to the hotel.

All the way back, we expressed our gratefulness to Rugie and Daphne for taking us to meet her friend in Brufut Marimma village. They both smiled and said, "Thank you for letting us take you out there." They said it as if we had done them a great favor. Again, I felt humble.

Meanwhile, Birdie gave them the specifics of our departure and schedule for the next day. "We're booked to go from Banjul back to Dakar where, after a short layover, we'll board our international flight to New York City," Birdie explained.

Both of their faces lit up and they said, "We will take you to the airport."

Of course, we consented excitedly as Rugie's husband drove into the driveway at the hotel.

We bade them farewell with the assurance that we'd see one another at least one more time the next morning.

To a Gambian Wrestling Match with Udomomu

Birdie and I strolled into the lobby of the hotel and took seats near a window where we'd have clear vision of the driveway.

It was almost magical that we'd gotten back from the village only a few minutes before a late-model Mercedes-Benz rolled into the driveway. A robust gentleman got out of the car and started walking toward the hotel lobby. As he approached us, Birdie and I exclaimed almost in duet, "What a coincidence and surprise! That's the man whose wife hosted us at lunch in their home with him and his driver when we were here in Banjul last year."

"I wonder if he'll remember us," Birdie asked me as he walked toward us with his arms outstretched. There was that familiar broad smile on his face. At that point, there was no doubt in my mind but that, indeed, he did remember us.

"It's Udomomu! It's Udomomu!" we called out. We all embraced one another.

"The McIntoshes," he repeated several times as he looked us up and down. He then ushered us into the backseat of his car. He got in behind the wheel.

"What an honor that you remember us! And what a coincidence that you would be assigned to take us to the wrestling matches!" we exclaimed.

As he drove off, he said, in typical pedagogical tone, "This is not at all a coincidence. I recognized your names on the manifest, and I purposely took the assignment to be your guide." I remembered then that when we met on our Pilgrimage, he told me that he had been a schoolteacher.

"You see, I planned this as an event for two reasons. Since I had the pleasure of hosting you on your previous visit, I wanted you to feel comfortable with some-one you knew to take you to the wrestling matches on this visit. And also, I would have the rare pleasure of being in your company again, because I consider you to be my friends," he said in that typical pedagogical tone of voice.

By now, neither Birdie nor I was coherent. We just sat there jabbering back and forth to him and then to each other. Just think, he had planned this reunion so thoughtfully and skillfully for our comfort and convenience. Again, my heart pounded with pride. I had a warm feeling of attachment to another member of my African family. I sat back and relaxed.

He drove only a short distance before we were at the entrance to the arena. After he let us out of the car, I noticed that he stepped in front of us. We followed him to the admission booth where he apparently paid our admission fee. He then led us to the outdoor arena. As we got closer and closer, I could hear the drums and intermittent roars from the crowd. When we got into the arena, I could see the wrestling area was roped off. An energetic match was already in progress.

He led us to the bleachers and sat between Birdie and me. As soon as I sat down, I realized that the bleachers were bare wood, because it felt hard to my bottom. I was surprised that there were so many people there, though mostly young people. Some were standing alongside the ring as close as they could get to the wrestlers. Some were sitting, and some were standing in the bleachers. They were all shouting and cheering.

The wrestlers were husky, well-developed, muscular male athletes with rapid footwork. They shuffled and maneuvered masterfully around the ring. The tops of their bodies were bare and glistening with sweat as if they had been greased. They might have been, but I didn't think to ask. All of them were clad in skimpy briefs. Other competitors were on the sidelines doing their warm-ups for upcoming matches.

The drumming was loud and continuous. Spectators, those seated in the bleachers and those standing on the sidelines around the arena, were wildly clapping their hands, yelling, and rooting for their favorite contender. They were stamping their feet and encouraging the wrestlers with jeers, whistles, and shouts. It was obvious that they loved the sport.

We sat quietly and watched. Because it was hard for me to tell when one match ended and another match began, I shouted to Udomomu, "What will be the winning feat?"

Above the din, he shouted back his answer, "When one wrestler's shoulder touches the ground or his opponent lifts him off his feet and throws him down, the match is over."

Since the crowd was so feverishly cheering for their favorite wrestlers, we couldn't talk, so I just sat there and watched. We stayed for two or three more of what I would call "matches."

At a lull in one of the matches, Udomomu asked us, "Will you ladies have a snack and a beverage with me before I take you back to the Badala?"

We were gracious and accepted, although I really wanted to get back to the hotel so I could go to bed and get some rest. Almost immediately after he asked us that, we left the arena and walked back to the car. The sun had gone down by this time, so it wasn't so hot.

So he wouldn't hear me, I told Birdie in a whispered tone as we were getting back into the car, "Now I've satisfied my curiosity about these wrestling matches we've heard so much about."

"Me too," she whispered back.

I was dead tired, but we went along with Udomomu's invitation. He took us to an establishment that resembled a cocktail lounge or supper club in America where hors-d'oeuvres and spirits were served. A small instrumental ensemble was performing. While we pigged out on the nibbles, sipped our spirits and chatted with Udomom and the bartender, several gentlemen came over and greeted us. Evidently they knew Udomom, because there was jovial congeniality among them. Also, even though their conversation was in Wolof, their body language led me to believe that they wanted to meet and chat with Birdie and me. A thought came to my mind, *It never fails. When Africans see us African Americans, they are drawn to us as if we're magnetized.*

He introduced us to them and translated their comments which were complimentary. But when we told him we were ready to go back to the hotel, he promptly but proudly excused us from the group, and the three of us left the lounge.

On the way back, we thanked him for his kindnesses and expressed our sincere appreciation for his having arranged this surprise reunion and for his sharing his time with us.

Upon arriving back at the hotel and just before parting, I reiterated my admiration for this unexpected renewal of our acquaintance with him, which he himself had purposefully orchestrated.

While I was talking to him, I was struck with the realization that in all likelihood, I'd never see him again.

Quickly but fondly, we bade each other farewell with best wishes and warm hugs. He turned and walked away. He got into his car, and as he drove off, we waved good-bye to him.

Birdie and I went to the pool area and ordered some refreshments before we took that long walk back to our room to pack for departure the next morning.

While we were watching some low-key poolside entertainment, a gentleman walked up to us and called us by name. "The McIntoshes from California and Ohio," he said ever so confidently.

When I took a good look at his face, I remembered him from the year before. To my amazement, it was the owner of the Badala Park Hotel. We had met him the year before, and he remembered us.

"We're impressed that you remember us and our names," we both stumbled out.

"That is my business," he said proudly. "It is good to have you back with us in The Gambia and especially here at the Badala Park Hotel. I hope you ladies are enjoying your visit."

Before we had a chance to answer, he said, "Remember, if there is anything I can do to make your stay more pleasurable, just let me know."

"Oh yes indeed, we're enjoying our stay here, even though it's been for just a few days this time," we said to him.

"I'm happy. I'm happy. Please come back again and again. Now may I offer you both a complimentary beverage?" he asked.

"Yes, and thank you for your hospitality," we answered.

He turned and walked away.

Very shortly, a server appeared at our table to take our orders.

The server said, "The owner of the hotel has asked me to serve you whatever it is you would like to have as refreshments from the bar. What would you like?"

While we sipped our refreshments, we remarked that there were so many swimmers in the pool so late in the day. They were playing pool games and socializing with one another, bouncing up and down in the water. When they came out of the pool, they continued to socialize unabashedly with other swimmers and guests who were lounging in the pool area. What I noticed mostly was that most of the women swimmers were topless.

Then and there, I had to admit to myself that perhaps my Western upbringing had insulated me with narrow-mindedness in this right of conduct. For a moment, I labored over whether it was right or wrong for those women swimmers to be exposing that part of their bodies as they bounced up and down in the pool, and then to see that they had the nerve to come out of the water in that "condition."

But the ambience of my immediate surroundings and the beauty and richness of my total experience overpowered my propensity to judge on the basis of my own moral values. I dismissed the thought from my mind, concluding that Western customs were unquestionably not universal.

After we finished our refreshments, we decided to take that long walk to our room which was located in the very furthest wing of the hotel. I was relieved that our room was on the ground level. At least we didn't have to climb any steps, because there was no elevator in that hotel.

We packed up our belongings and made ready for the bellman to pick up our luggage the next morning.

Before rolling into my bed, I took out my journal and with a full heart, made significant notes.

Back Home to America

Soon after our continental breakfast in the hotel, Rugie and the family arrived to take us to the airport. We climbed into the back of the truck. Rugie's husband put our luggage back there with us, and we took off.

Just as we turned onto the main street leading away from the hotel, we encountered some sort of gala festival or observance in progress on the main thoroughfare. Therefore, several of the streets were roped off from traffic. Because of that, Rugie explained that her husband would have to take a detour. I didn't know the difference, so it was all right with me. I just settled back and took one long, last look at Serrekunda, The Gambia, West Africa.

It seemed we were all in a pensive mood, because there wasn't much conversation. Smiling at each other, we just jostled along in the back of the pickup. I tried to soak up as much character of the atmosphere as I could during those last few moments. The question was churning in my head, *Will this be the last time I get to be with my family in The Gambia?*

Out of the blue, Rugie said, "Sister Jane and Sister Birdie, we feel like you are a part of our family, and we hope you feel the same way about us. We are all a part of each other's family, you know."

We shared our sentiments with them as we jostled along. Daphne and Rugie had always lovingly called me "Big Sis," even though I'm old enough to be their grandmother, and Isha's great-grandmother. As usual, I had to fight back the tears, but I managed to maintain my composure and just treasure their sentiments.

When we arrived at the airport, we said our tearful good-byes as we got out of the back of the truck with our baggage.

It's observably conspicuous but customary for natives to only be allowed within a certain distance of the entrance to the airport terminals. I guess it's because some natives have been able to slip through security.

Just before taking our positions in line to surrender our documents, we embraced, turned and waved our final goodbyes to Rugie, her husband, Daphne, and Isha.

My heart sank as I watched them walk away with their heads bowed.

Wrestling with all of our luggage, Birdie and I got in line, expecting to have our luggage checked when our tickets and passports were submitted to the authorities.

We stood in one spot for such a long time, and the line wasn't moving, so we approached an airport employee who was walking toward us. Fortunately, he spoke English. We asked him what we were doing wrong.

He never really stopped walking, but he told us we weren't doing anything wrong. He nonchalantly told us that the reason the line wasn't moving was because documents weren't yet being processed since the plane we were supposed to catch had not arrived from Abidjan. He kept walking.

Of course, our next question was, "When will the plane arrive?"

Over his shoulder, he answered, "I do not know."

Needless to say, we were disappointed and frantically countered, "But we need to get to Dakar to catch our flight to JFK in New York."

Upon further inquiry, he stopped walking and told us that the reason for the extended delay was that the pilot in Banjul, who was assigned to fly us to Dakar, had not yet arrived for duty. Between those two explanations, we resigned ourselves to just relax and wait to see what the next explanation would be.

By that time, the line had dispersed, and fuming passengers were all just milling around in the terminal and outside the entrance.

Birdie said, "Well, we might as well wait outside, Jane."

"Right," I agreed.

Our family was standing there in the distance, watching, so we waved to them as we all walked toward each other. When we joined, we all got some snacks and beverages while we told them of our plight.

Birdie exclaimed optimistically, "But unexpectedly, we're able to enjoy a little more time together!"

Cynically, I told Birdie, "I get the feeling that this isn't an unusual occurrence—the plane from Abidjan being delayed."

"But can you imagine a pilot not yet showing up for work?" Birdie countered.

"I've never heard of such a thing in America," I grumbled.

Standing there with our friends, we stayed within viewing distance of the entrance to the terminal in order to see when the line started forming again. In the meantime, we took a picture of the family.

Our Family in The Gambia

"Keep working on getting a visa to come to visit us," Birdie said to the girls as we munched our goodies.

"Oh, we will, we will," they assured us.

Rugie excitedly said, "I'm going to send you some things when you get back to America."

"That'll be wonderful!" Birdie replied.

I was pondering why they would spend their money to buy something to send to us. We were much more able to send something to them.

About that time, we noticed that a boarding line had formed again and was already moving, but very slowly. So we hugged one another and said our farewells again.

Birdie and I left them standing there. They were wearing happy faces, covering up what I believed were their true feelings. Just before clearing the entrance to the terminal, we turned and waved our final last good-byes.

We inched along to approach the immigration officer to get our documents processed so we could board our short flight to Dakar.

Finally, we boarded. The flight was short and uneventful, except for the irate remarks and conversations we overheard among English-speaking passengers.

They were all bemoaning the fact that, like us, they would miss their connecting flights to JFK.

Of course, Birdie and I were in the same predicament, but in her usual calm voice, she said, "Well, Jane, we'll miss our flight, too, but there's nothing we can do about it."

When we landed, there was a mad rush for the terminal. It was almost like a stampede. The other passengers were reacting fervently to their plight. But Birdie and I took our time and leisurely walked into the terminal to get in line to board whatever flight we could get to JFK.

Much to my surprise, when we walked in, we sensed that something catastrophic had occurred there. Just as we got further inside, I heard an announcement over the public address system. The message was that the flight had been delayed.

We looked at each other in amazement, saying, "No, not again."

At that point, most passengers were literally in a state of rage and furor, except one gentleman in particular, whom I observed. He was tall and slender with that regal posture. I think he was Senegalese. He took long strides as he walked over to an isolated spot in a corner away from the crowd of enraged passengers. Slowly, he untied his prayer rug, carefully spread it out on the floor, and turned around very deliberately to face what I guess was the east. He knelt down on his rug. His body language led me to believe that he was praying.

I found it comforting to see how that man was coping with the predicament he faced at that time. I didn't know him, but I admired him. What I saw was a sterling symbol of accepting circumstances that we cannot change.

All the while, nearly everybody else was shamelessly voicing their fury over the fact that this flight had also been delayed. Since many passengers were African American, their almost hysterical comments were loud and unabashed. They were walking back and forth, venting their wrath, disapproval, and rage, all directed at the employees of Air Afrique. Some were demanding an answer to their questions, such as "Why is this flight delayed?" … "I'm supposed to be back at work tomorrow morning." … "What am I going to do?"

Birdie and I just stood there in awe, watching the tirade.

In my mind, I could hear Madame Gueye telling us that her husband told her to ask us about the quality of service provided by Air Afrique. It was then that I think I grasped the underlying reason for his asking. It was probably that he had heard rumors of recent problems that passengers were experiencing while traveling via Air Afrique.

To even further irritate passengers, a female employee was walking down our line, demanding that we surrender our passports to her. When she got to us, I asked, "Why do I have to surrender my passport?"

She stated, "I am going to make a copy of it and then return it to you."

Birdie asked, "Why do you need to make a copy of our passports?"

Rather curtly, she replied, "It is for security reasons."

In spite of our indignation, of course, we handed her our passports. She continued down the line, collecting passports from passengers who were standing in line behind us.

We discussed our circumstances, but came to the logical conclusion that there wasn't anything we could do if we wanted to be processed to board our flight whenever it departed so we could get back home. Realizing that it would be quite a while before she got back to us with our passports, we walked around the terminal and browsed in the gift shop.

Soon thereafter, she returned our passports to us. In my rage, I told her that when I returned to my office, I was going to report the incident to the Department of State in Washington, DC. She made no comment or showed any sign of concern whatsoever. She just continued down the line, returning passports to the passengers.

Finally, we boarded our flight for New York City. The flight was an anticlimax after all we'd been through both in the Banjul and Dakar air terminals.

Having been so vexed by the delay in departures, it was with dread and mental suffering that we called Gaines and Arthur. Birdie placed the call from the nearest phone booth to advise them that we'd have to reschedule our flight from New York to Cincinnati by whatever accommodations we could get.

When she handed the phone to me, I apologetically told Gaines of our plight and said, "When we make new reservations, we'll call you to let you know our new travel plans and when to pick us up."

"No problem," Gaines said in his usual reassuring tone of voice. "Just let us know, and we'll be there."

With a heavy heart, I hung up the phone. We walked to the ticket counter and presented our connecting flight tickets. The gentleman at the counter confirmed that the flight on which we were scheduled to depart had taken off long ago.

"I can book you on a flight to Philadelphia and then a flight from Philadelphia to Cincinnati if you like. The flight to Philadelphia will depart in forty-five minutes," he said.

In desperation, we both agreed, "That'll be just fine."

He was gracious and accommodating. "Since your departing flight from Leopold Senghor Airport in Dakar to JFK in New York was unavoidably delayed, many passengers have requested rerouting. There'll be no additional charge for you since the delay was no fault of yours."

"Thank you! Thank you!" we chimed simultaneously as he handed us our tickets to Cincinnati through Philadelphia.

Birdie went immediately to the phone booth to call Gaines and Arthur to let them know the details of our rerouting and arrival time in Cincinnati.

We boarded our flight to Philadelphia. To my dismay, the plane was much smaller than I had anticipated. We hadn't thought to ask, and it hadn't been pointed out to us when we were rerouted. Nevertheless, we boarded and were seated across the aisle from each other. The plane had nine seats on each side of the aisle and two seats up front for two pilots. In fact, the plane was so small that I could see the pilots from my seat for the short forty-five-minute flight from New York to Philadelphia.

It seemed that we soared just above the telephone poles. All the way, I could actually see the telephone wires just below us. The roar of the engine was noticeable, but from across the aisle, we spent those few minutes cogitating whether or not our luggage had been transferred when we were rerouted. In our zeal, we neglected to check on those specifics, so we left it to fate. Shortly, we landed.

We seated ourselves at the gate in Philadelphia, waiting for our flight to Cincinnati.

Conversation lulled and fatigue set in for me. "I'm exhausted," I said to Birdie.

"Situations such as this are exhausting," she said in her usual comforting tone. "Are you all right?"

"Yes, I'm OK, just tired and frustrated," I reassured her. Again, I appreciated her care and concern.

Very shortly, our flight was called, and we got in line to board for the last lap of our journey on our mission. Almost as soon as we were airborne, we were served beverages. Equally as soon as we took our last swallow, the receptacles were collected in preparation for landing in Cincinnati.

Surely enough, Gaines and Arthur were at the gate to welcome us back to America. I was so glad to see them that I fell into their arms with blessed relief from the return travel ordeal we had been through. All the way to baggage claim, I was particularly selective in sharing with Gaines only the colossal, triumphant events of our "mission," saving my disapproving recount of the downside and negative events for later.

I postponed sharing events that began with the episode of our being left alone in that hot car at the border between Senegal and The Gambia while Ramou negotiated with the border patrol officer. And then there was our woeful tale about the fiascoes with our flight delays on Air Afrique in both Banjul and Dakar.

I dreaded the possibility that Gaines might remind me of his earliest admonition, "Jane, you haven't got any business going to Africa. You don't know anything about Africa, and you don't know anything about those people."

I really didn't want to hear him say that to me again.

We left the terminal, and Arthur loaded the trunk of the car with our baggage. All the way home, I tried to remain bubbly and upbeat about our experiences in general, purposely leaving out the specifically abhorrent details because the down-side definitely did not cast a blight on the richness and magnificence of my total experience. I still felt abundantly blessed to have been able to make the journey back to my Motherland. Birdie and I had completed our mission.

Before I realized it, Arthur was pulling up in front of the house. We all settled in for the night after the tasty familiar American cuisine Arthur had prepared for our welcome-home dinner.

Gaines and I spent New Year's Eve and New Year's Day with Art and Birdie and the kids. The next day, we left for our home in dear old Hayward, California, USA. During our flight, I shared some more of my joyful experiences with him and basked in the enchantment he showed while relating the pleasures I had enjoyed on our mission.

Several days later, when I had mustered up enough courage to tell him about our fiascoes, as anticipated, he jokingly reminded me, "Jane, I told you that you had no business going to Africa, because you didn't know anything about Africa, and you didn't know anything about 'those people'."

"But, Gaines, the positives far outweighed the negatives," I convinced him.

"Right. I must admit that now you know about Africa and 'those people'." I'm glad you went, Jane, and I know you'll cherish your experiences for the rest of your life. "I'm just glad you made it home safely," he said as if he felt relieved.

"I missed you at Christmas, and I hope we'll not be apart again on Christmas," I said.

"Me, too," he answered, as we cuddled.

My Naming Ceremony

The First Lap of My Journey

After several hectic days of preparation and planning, on the fifteenth of February, 2001, I joyously boarded my flight in San Francisco for JFK in New York. There, I would join Mamadou and Suweeyah for our well-planned journey to Dakar for my naming ceremony. The flight was smooth and relaxing.

When I arrived at JFK, I couldn't remember how to get from the domestic terminal to the international terminal. Instinctively, I stopped suddenly and looked around for someone I could ask.

I said to myself, *Oh, there's a skycap.* He was loading another passenger's luggage onto a cart.

I approached him and said, "Excuse me, sir, but could you please tell me how to get to the international terminal?"

He looked up at me and asked, "Which airline do you want, ma'am?"

Proudly, I told him, "Air Afrique."

In a helpful tone, he answered with a slight foreign accent, "Walk over to the baggage carousel. I'll be back in a few minutes. Then I will take you to the international terminal. If your baggage comes around, just leave it there, and I will pull it off for you when I get back."

I thanked him. As I walked over to the baggage carousel, I had a fleeting skepticism as to whether or not he really would come back. But, instantly, my perpetual faith pervaded. My inherent optimism dispelled skepticism.

He left the area, pushing his cart which was loaded with baggage. His passenger was following close behind him.

I sauntered over to the baggage claim carousel and watched for my luggage and the package I had checked. In a few minutes, the skycap returned and almost at the same time, my luggage and the package came around together on the carousel. I identified my two pieces. He pulled them off and put them on his cart.

"Did you say you need to go to Air Afrique?" he asked.

"Yes, I'm going to Dakar, Senegal," I told him.

He put my belongings onto his cart. In a reassuring tone of voice, he said, "Follow me. I will take you to Air Afrique."

I trotted along behind him. Off and on, he looked back and realized that I wasn't walking as fast as he was. Noticeably, he slowed down a bit. The thought ran through my mind, *He has an accent that reminds me of some Africans' accents.*

As I caught up with him, I asked, "What country are you from?"

"I'm from Barbados," he replied, "So you're going to Dakar?"

"Yes, for the third time," I proudly answered him.

He said no more, so I just kept walking close behind him. When we arrived in the Air Afrique boarding area, I said, "Thank you for your help."

He unloaded the cart and set my luggage and package at my feet.

With a slight bow as he accepted his gratuity, he smiled and said, "Thank you very much. Enjoy your trip." He disappeared.

I scanned the area and caught sight of Mamadou and Suweeyah. Right away, I heard voices calling out to me, "Mum Jane! Mum Jane!" There they were, coming toward me.

We all embraced, and I relaxed into the arms of my African family.

Absentmindedly, I forgot about my baggage and left it setting there. In his take-charge manner, Mamadou went back and got my baggage. Suweeyah and I followed him to the area where they had been seated before I arrived.

As we walked, she brought me up to date by telling me that they had followed their original plan to spend the previous night in New York. She said they had gotten up early, gone to the terminal, and had been in the Air Afrique boarding area since noon.

I relaxed into a seat. As I heaved a sigh of relief, a gentleman who was sitting there in the next seat down the row, stood up. Mamadou faced me and motioned toward the gentleman. Directing the introduction to me, he said, "Mum Jane, this is another Mamadou."

Directing the introduction to the other Mamadou, he said, "This is Mum Jane from California, my *sama yaye* (other mother), whom I was telling you about."

With typical Senegalese English articulation, the gentleman smiled as he rose from his seat, "Hello, Mum Jane. It is nice to meet you."

Directing his comment back to me, Mamadou added, "This gentleman is my countryman. But we just met each other when we got here. He is going home to visit his family in Dakar. I have invited him to your naming ceremony."

I acknowledged the introduction.

Knowing that Gaines had been ill for quite some time and that I was his primary care provider, with an intense expression on his face, Mamadou immediately asked, "How is Father Gaines?" (That's what Mamadou had called Gaines ever since he was our houseguest in Hayward soon after he left Senegal to join his wife who was African American and lived in Maple Heights, Ohio.)

I told them Gaines was about the same and that he still had his medical challenges.

With the same intense expression, Mamadou asked, "Who is taking care of him while you are away?"

I explained to them, "Gaines's doctors insisted that I take some time off for my own health and well-being. They were exceptionally helpful in advising and assisting me in making and carrying out our plans and arrangements for his care while I'd be away. Therefore, I hired a twenty-four-hour caregiver to live in and take care of him. She is a very competent young woman who is an experienced nursing assistant. She was handpicked for the assignment. Furthermore, she is the granddaughter of very dear friends of ours. And in addition to her daily attendant care, she'll be supervised by a registered nurse who will come every other day to guide, monitor, and evaluate the quality of care she provides. Both of us, as well as his doctors, are confident that he'll be well taken care of while I'm away."

All during my monologue, the three of them were nodding their heads in what appeared to be silent approval of my explanation.

About 6:30 PM, an Air Afrique agent appeared behind the podium at the check-in counter. I was surprised that there was no mad rush to the counter to check in. So we leisurely lined up and waited for the agent to recognize us. I found myself first in line. Suweeyah was right behind me, then Mamadou behind her, and then his countryman right behind Mamadou. Other passengers began to line up by twos and threes behind us.

Just then, a young woman, trying to comfort her crying babe in arms, stepped ahead of me. I could see that she was stressed out. I sympathized with her.

As we watched the agent setting up for passenger checking-in, Suweeyah told me that a couple of hours before noon, she and Mamadou had checked out of the hotel. She said they came directly to the airport and had been in the Air Afrique boarding area since right after they had lunch in the terminal.

While we stood there in line just talking, a young man caught my eye because he was dressed in some kind of airline service uniform. He was sitting behind the baggage scales. His demeanor and appearance was so languid and indolent, it was impossible not to take note of him. His head and body were keeping time to music blasting from a small boom box on the floor beside him. In fact, I thought his presence and demeanor, as well as the genre and volume of the music were inappropriate for an airline boarding area. I mentioned it to Suweeyah. She agreed, and we went on talking.

After the mother and her child were checked in, the agent motioned for me to step up to the counter. I stepped up, presented my documents, and watched as she scrutinized them. She then told me to set my baggage up on the scale.

I told her, "I'm sorry, but I can't lift it. It's too heavy for me. Do you have someone who could do that for me?" Silently, I was alluding to the young man who was sitting behind the scales.

Indignantly, she said something to him in a foreign language.

In a sullen manner, the young man stood up and sauntered over, picked up my baggage and put each piece on the scale. He then disappeared through the exit behind the check-in counter.

The agent returned my passport, stapled two baggage claim checks to the inside pocket of my folder and tucked my ticket back into the pocket, along with my boarding pass. I thanked her and turned away from the counter. When the other three in our group had been processed, we decided to have something to eat before boarding. They told me that it was just a short walk to the escalator, which would take us to a Chinese buffet on the second floor.

Full of good food and beverages, we got back in line to go to the boarding gate. Finally, we boarded.

Mamadou and Suweeyah's seats were side-by-side on the opposite side from where I was seated on the plane. In fact, we couldn't even see each other. I felt lonely and my thoughts turned to Gaines.

As I securely fastened my seat belt, I relaxed and settled in with my reading materials, readily accessible in my carry-on bag. The flight attendants began performing their duties. As I looked around, it flashed through my mind that on my first Air Afrique flight, one of the attendants informed me that the aircraft was an airbus, and it was "owned by Africa."

Our ascent was normal, but as we got out over the Atlantic Ocean, the flight became disturbingly turbulent. Then as we climbed higher and higher, the plane began to rock back and forth. I became petrified. I tried to sit motionless, clutching the armrests, hoping that would allay my fear.

I looked around again and saw my same fear on the faces of all of the other passengers within my view. Since my seat was over on the other side of the plane and not even close to Mamadou and Suweeyah, I had no comfort from being close to anyone who cared about me. Even though it wouldn't have done any good, I consciously yearned for someone with whom I could share my fear.

All the while, the plane was shaking, and at frequent intervals it plummeted up and down, up and down. Unable to stay in my seat even though I had my belt securely fastened, I was terrified. I felt hopelessly helpless. Uncontrollably, I screamed.

But I wasn't the only one who was screaming. It sounded as if everybody aboard was screaming. I even heard male voices among the screams. That terrified me even more, because I'd never heard men scream from fear before. I couldn't help looking around and seeing utter fear and panic on the faces of all other passengers around me.

Finally, the captain came on the address system and told us that he had run into unusual turbulence. To me, it seemed almost ludicrous for him to finally say that, because we were all suffering from its effect. In the same announcement, he ordered everyone, including the attendants, to be seated and to keep our seat belts securely fastened. In an attempt to allay our fears, he told us that he was going to drop his altitude, hoping he could get below the turbulence.

We rocked and rolled out over the Atlantic Ocean for every bit of twenty to thirty terrifying minutes, which seemed like an eternity to me. Every now and then when the turbulence got rougher, we were all screaming, terrorized with fear of the worst that could happen—that Air Afrique's airbus enroute to Dakar, Senegal, West Africa, would plunge into the Atlantic Ocean with all of us aboard, crying and screaming.

My thoughts flashed prayerfully to dear Gaines. I prayed like I had never prayed before—that God would keep me safe so I could go back home and take care of Gaines. And I believe God answered my prayer, because we gradually flew out of the turbulence. The flight smoothed out, and the passengers settled down.

With instructions from the pilot, the attendants resumed their routine and served us a meal, along with a bottle of dry red wine. I needed both.

When we landed in Dakar, I was so nervous and edgy, I was like a zombie. I got on the first motor coach I saw, only to discover that I had lost sight of Mamadou and Suweeyah. For a moment, I felt stranded and abandoned. I almost panicked but had sense enough left to realize that they had either caught a motor coach in front of the one I got on or they had gotten onto one that was following mine. So I just rode and thanked God for getting us across the Atlantic and back on land, any land.

The bus stopped, and I got off. I stood there a moment and saw Mamadou and Suweeyah getting off of the bus behind mine. They came to help me with my carry-on, and we walked to the front of the terminal to go through immigration.

But before we even got inside, I saw a throng of people standing in a group. Of course, they all rushed to Mamadou.

His family and friends embraced. They all broke down in tears, and as they sobbed, they held onto one another as if for dear life. Tears were streaming down their cheeks. Others gathered around them as they held onto one another. Everyone was unabashedly crying, sharing in the joy of their reunion with Mamadou.

I froze in my tracks as I witnessed the most emotional homecoming experience of my life. That emotional demonstration of love and devotion brought tears to my eyes too, just being in the company of his family and friends who had come to welcome him home. Because it was the first time he'd been able to return since he married and left Dakar to join his wife in America, it was obvious that they had been joyfully awaiting this homecoming. Such a sincere outpouring of joy and love I had never experienced before, nor have I had another such experience since that day.

After we regained some composure, we went inside to get processed through immigration. As we walked, family and friends were saying, "Welcome home! Welcome home!"

Just then, I saw Madame Gueye smiling as she walked up to me and put her arm around my waist. We embraced. She said, "Welcome home, Jane. I'll be taking you home with me to be my houseguest while you are here in Dakar for your naming ceremony."

We went through immigration and then on to baggage claim. The process went smoothly, with no hang-ups. A friend of Mamadou's assisted with my luggage and the package I had checked. He walked with Madame Gueye and me to her car. It was parked not very far away from the terminal exit. We all got in for the ride to her home.

When we got there, Madame Gueye showed the helper to my room down the hall. It was the same room Birdie and I occupied when we were in Dakar for Mamadou's wedding. He took my luggage in and set it down.

Lastly, he brought the package in from the car, and when he got to the doorway of the living room, I directed him not to take the package to my room but to set it in the living room.

She didn't say anything, but Madame Gueye looked at me with a querying expression.

I thanked the helper. He said good night and left.

Madame Gueye slipped out of her shoes. I followed suit and slipped out of my shoes. She led me into the living room. I sat down on the sofa and told her that the package was for her.

Smilingly, she took a long look at me. Excitedly, she asked, "For me? For me?"

"Yes, for you," I answered.

When she had torn off the wrapping paper, she read the labeling on the manufacturer's packing carton.

She shouted with glee, "Oh, Jane, you brought me a microwave oven. Thank you! Thank you! Thank you!"

Through her exclamations of joy, I reminded her, "When you visited Gaines and me in Hayward, I promised to send a microwave oven to you as a gift. But since I was never able to make the satisfactory shipping arrangements, I decided to bring it with me when I came for my naming ceremony. That way, I could present it to you in person."

I told her she would need to convert the plug to her local electrical current.

She assured me in her methodical diction, "Oh yes, I know. That is no problem. I will have my son take it to the electrician in the original packing carton and have it converted. Thank you! Thank you! Thank you!"

"I'm glad to know that won't be a problem for you."

My heart pounded as I recognized how much more momentous it was for us to be together when she opened her gift. I realized too that this was another one of God's preordained events for the two of us.

"I want you to know how honored I am for you to have invited me to be your houseguest again," I reminded her.

By now, it was the wee hours of the morning. After some small talk, we bade each other good night and went to our bedrooms. Before I shut down for the night, I hastily made notes in my journal before I went to sleep.

A Revealing Cross-cultural Dialogue

I slept well. In fact, I slept so well, it was almost two o'clock in the afternoon when I awakened. As soon as I emerged from my room the house helpers brought out a fresh-baked baguette of French bread, cut-up melon and fruit, some thinly sliced cheese, and coffee. As they set the breakfast foods on the table, Madame Gueye and I sat down.

She scooted her chair up to the table, laid the palm of her hand on my arm, smiled at me and said, "Jane, I want to thank you again for the gift you brought me."

"You're most welcome, Madame Gueye, and I hope you enjoy using it as much as you enjoyed using mine when you visited us in Hayward," I reminded her.

We munched on our continental breakfast. I enjoyed the breakfast food even though it was the middle of the day.

"What would you like to do the rest of today?" she asked me.

Caught by surprise, I replied, "Whatever you decide to do, I know I'll enjoy doing it with you."

With that, she told me, "I would like for you to meet some more of my family members. Also, I would like for you to meet my mother and daughter neighbors who just recently bought the house next door. The mother, who is my friend, is a dentist. She asked me to tell you that since she has appointments on Monday, she will not be able to attend your naming ceremony."

When we finished our meal and got up from the table, intriguingly, she said, "Come with me."

With that, she led me out the door to the sidewalk and over to the house next door. She rapped lightly on the door. While we waited for the door to open, she told me, "My friend's daughter has spent a good deal of time in America and is anxious to meet you and talk with you. Also, she speaks very good English."

Madame Gueye barely got the words out of her mouth when the door opened. We were greeted by a lady who had a bright smile on her face. Recalling from my rusty college French, I understood her saying, *"Entrez-vous. entrez-vous,"* as she welcomed us into her home. Madame Gueye introduced me.

She was a poised, positive, confident, middle-aged woman who was fluent in English. Her outward appearance was typical of what I've observed about most Senegalese women whom I've met.

Without my asking, she voluntarily took me on a grand tour of the house. I wondered if she had the false impression that I had come to scrutinize her home and compare it with Madame Gueye's home. I dismissed that thought from my mind and reconciled it by acknowledging the fact that this woman did not know me at all. The tour revealed that this was a large custom-built, roomy house with airy, spacious rooms, lots of windows, and glossy, refurbished floors throughout. It also had an attached two-car garage.

She apologized for the sparsely furnished living room. That room impressed me right away since I don't relate to overfurnishing. I secretly wanted to tell her not to put a piece of furniture on every square foot of floor space in the room. It would only detract from its spaciousness and airiness and the beauty of the grains in the wood flooring.

In spite of the fact that I had just met her, I felt comfortable enough to venture to say, "If you don't put any more furniture in here, it would suit me just fine."

However, she continued to apologize. She was quick to add that she hadn't been in the house very long and was still in the throes of decorating.

After the tour, she invited me to sit down on a big soft sofa. I sank into the soft cushion upholstered in a warm, dark print fabric. Madame Gueye sat down beside me. Her friend sat in a matching chair opposite us.

Madame Gueye sat with us for just a few minutes. Then she got up and said, "I am going home to do a few things, but I will be back in a little while." She walked to the front door and let herself out.

Her neighbor and I immediately began getting acquainted. I told her I was a violinist and a retired instrumental music teacher, having taught in both public and private schools and privately in my own studio in my home.

She interrupted me and said, "Madame Gueye has told us all about you and that she had been the guest of you and your husband in your beautiful home in California."

It was true that Madame Gueye had told her all about me, because it was at this point that she congratulated me for having written and published a book about my pilgrimage to Senegal and The Gambia.

She smiled as she told me how proud Madame Gueye had been to have me as her houseguest on my last visit for Mamadou's wedding.

My ears perked up when she shared the fact that she had spent several years working in the corporate world in America. She said that she was currently on a one-year leave of absence from her position and had returned to Senegal to spend time with her family.

She told me that her corporate experience had been incredibly rewarding financially and that she had richly benefited from the opportunity to live and work in America.

With just a cursory glance at some of the amenities and appointments in her home, it was apparent to me that she had wisely invested her financial resources.

She shared with me the information that while working in America, she had been supervised by a gentleman who had relocated there from Germany some twenty-five years before. She praised him as her supervisor and said she greatly respected him because he pushed her to climb the corporate ladder of success through promotions within the company.

"As a result, in addition to my own comfortable lifestyle, I have been financially able to pay for my daughter's education in Montreal," she said almost boastfully.

She placed emphasis on the fact that her daughter was fluent in both French and English, one of the strong advantages of having been born and reared in Senegal where both languages were taught and spoken. She said that since leaving college in Montreal, her daughter had worked in Washington, DC. She didn't elaborate as to where her daughter worked or what she did in DC, but I surmised that her position was professional.

At that point and rather pensively, she added that as she climbed the corporate ladder of success in America, at each rung she had questioned herself as to whether or not she was becoming westernized and quasimaterialistic.

She said, "There, I felt that the focus boiled down to be all about making money and in some instances, regardless of ethical values." All in the same breath, she said, "Thankfully, that is not my hereditary frame of reference. I love my heritage which is grounded in moral consequences, and I don't want to lose that quality."

With a facial expression of pure contentment, she smiled and said, "Since returning home, I have come to the conclusion that I definitely am not the type of person to continue to work and eventually retire in America. I have decided not to go back. I am content to be here at home in Dakar with my family. Dakar is where I belong."

"That's beautiful," I said "I can certainly respect your set of values. And you're absolutely right. You do, indeed, have to accept the fact that in order to establish and maintain a stable and secure lifestyle in America, it's paramount to concentrate on making money in order to survive and provide for your prosperity and peace of mind."

"I am content being back home here in Dakar with my family. But you know, Jane, since I've been back home, I've observed that the bonding structure of some families in Dakar is changing," she said. "I don't mean to imply that it has broken down, but it is definitely changing."

"Explain that to me," I asked.

"For example, there are many young Senegalese professionals who have studied and earned professional degrees in America. When they returned to Dakar, they found that others who are also professional and earning professional salaries are competing among one another for material things. Their values are beginning to parallel Western values," she elaborated.

I identified with her explanation but asked her, "Do you think that may be the result of their having spent a considerable length of time in America where materialism is ubiquitous? You know, all eyes are on America."

She responded, "That could very well be true." Then she went on to say, "However, it's still true that the elite groups of Senegalese people are the families of long-standing tradition. And their values are indelible."

"Can you elaborate on that a little bit?" I asked.

"Yes," she replied. "Senegalese people who bear certain family names are placed in a special class or group."

She didn't really answer my question, but I reflected on information Mamadou had imparted relative to family names. I construed her statement to mean that her family name placed her in one of those special classes or groups.

Just then, Madame Gueye came through the front door. We ended our conversation and all walked out of the house together and went back over to Madame Gueye's house.

The first thing Madame Gueye did when we came in was to show her friend her gift, the microwave oven I had brought her from America. It was apparent that her friend was happy for her but not bowled over with a microwave oven, which I knew was no novelty to a woman who had recently lived in America.

She stayed only a few minutes longer and graciously excused herself by saying, "I must leave in time to have dinner ready when my mother comes home from her office." As she left, she assured me, "But I'll see you at your naming ceremony."

I said to her as she stood at the door, "I look forward to seeing you there, but I want to tell you now that I consider it a distinct privilege to have met you, and I want to thank you for sharing your time with me this afternoon. I thoroughly enjoyed our visit."

She thanked me and quietly closed the door.

After she left, I was surprised and happy to renew acquaintance with one of Madame Gueye's sons and one of her daughters. Of course, they recognized me right away. They were friendly and cordial. Both of them spoke fluent English.

With true enthusiasm in his voice, her son spontaneously told me, "I've studied in America. As a matter of fact, I took some courses in French literature and aced every one of them."

His sister chimed in and said, "Yes, he did very well. There's a strong advantage in being bi-lingual, and especially in French and English."

"Congratulations to both of you and best wishes in all you do," I encouraged them.

They smiled and said, "Thank you. We'll be at your naming ceremony."

"Good! I'll be looking forward to seeing you there. Do you know where and when?"

"Oh, yes, we know everything about it," they answered almost in unison.

Madame Gueye said, "Come with me, Jane. I am going to the fruit market."

We hopped in the car, and she took off. She had driven only a short distance when she stopped in front of a huge outdoor fruit and vegetable market.

As we walked in, all of the merchants greeted her warmly, almost as if she were a celebrity. I had no doubt that she spent a lot of money in their markets, and they valued her as a regular customer. She seemed proud to introduce me to some of the merchants as her friend from California. I was happy to notice that among the things she picked up were melons and bananas. She bade them farewell. We left and rode back home.

One of her house helpers met us and opened the door. I could smell the makings of a meal being prepared. She handed the shopping bag to her house helper. The other one was on her way to the front of the house with the straw mat and damask tablecloth. She spread them out on the living room floor. In just a moment or two, the other house helper came out of the kitchen. She was carrying a large platter of food and she set it down on the tablecloth.

Following Madame Gueye's lead, I sat down on the floor, and we began our meal. The menu was fish, rice, salad, and French bread. I pigged out on the French bread which was light and fluffy like it is in France. We had iced bissap tea with our bananas and cut-up melon and fruit for dessert. While we ate, she asked me if I enjoyed my visit with her friend next door.

"Oh, yes, Madame Gueye. I can't thank you enough for providing such a rich exposure and contact for me," I said to her between chews. "She truly loves her homeland. It was a privilege to talk with a person who espouses such wholesome values. I hope to be able to spend time with her again some day."

She smiled and said, "We all hope the same thing. Tomorrow, I'm going to take you to meet some more of my family members. They're all coming to your naming ceremony. I especially want you to meet one of my aunts. She is planning her first trip to Mecca."

Just then, the phone rang. When she came back, she said the phone call was from Mamadou who offered to come over at ten o'clock in the morning to take us on a tour of the city, go to a museum, or whatever else we might decide to do.

My jet lag had caught up with me, so I told her I was going to bed. She said goodnight. I went to my room, took out my journal, and made lots of notes.

I thanked God for another day in my Motherland with my African family and then crawled into bed.

The Day Before My Special Day

The next morning after breakfast, we went outside and took pictures. While we were out there, Mamadou's niece arrived in a taxi. She said she had come to take me to her house to talk with her family about her coming to America to help me take care of Gaines. Some time before, we had briefly touched on the subject, and I was optimistic about the blessed opportunity with the possibility of getting a work visa for her to come and live with us.

I got into the taxi with her and on the way to Mamadou's house, I reopened the subject by asking her, "Have you ever been away from home before?"

She said she had not.

I thought for a moment as to how best to point out a few important facts to her since her lifestyle would be dramatically different from the lifestyle to which she was accustomed. I decided that this was the opportune time, so I turned and faced her as I admonished her, "Since you've never been away from home before, you'll miss your mother, your father, your grandmother, your sisters, your nieces, your nephews, and all of your extended family."

I also told her, "You will be a long, long way from home, and it costs a lot of money to travel back and forth. Therefore, you won't be able to make the trip back home whenever you get homesick."

She was silent as she listened when I told her, "Think it over carefully before you make your final decision to leave your country, even for a short while."

She broke her silence, looked me straight in the eyes and said, "I will be all right, especially since I will be living with you. And then, I can go to school."

I told her I'd need full consent from her family even before making any preliminary arrangements. But I promised her that if her family approved, I would go to the embassy the day after my naming ceremony, talk to the authorities there, and get all pertinent information, necessary forms and applications to start the process of getting a work visa for her.

By that time, we were pulling up in front of the house. We got out and went in where her grandmother, her mother, father, sisters and several little children were all gathered in the living room. They all said hello, but it appeared to me that they'd been prepped that a very important meeting was about to take place, because as soon as she and I entered the room, her mother, father, and grandmother led us into a large bedroom adjoining the living room.

We all sat down, and then I presented the proposition that I would apply for a work visa for her to come to Hayward. She would live with Gaines and me, help me take care of Gaines, and eventually apply for a student visa so she could go to school.

I got the distinct impression that they had thoroughly discussed the matter and agreed to permit her to accept the offer, because as soon as I had clearly presented the proposition, they unanimously granted permission for her to pursue my offer.

Of course, I was pleased beyond measure. It was not only a tailor-made solution to our dilemma but also anticipated that it provided an opportunity for her to live and eventually go to college in America.

"I sincerely thank all of you for your confidence in me and reassure you that Mr. McIntosh and I will do all we can for her while she's with us in Hayward," I said as we left the room.

We joined other family members in the living room. We were served pound cake and orange juice. The orange juice tasted freshly squeezed and like it had ginger in it. Soon afterward, Mamadou, Suweeyah, and Mamadou's brother came in together.

They invited me to lunch with them. Of course, I accepted their offer and bade everyone *au revoir*.

"We will go to a new restaurant. I heard it just opened not too long ago," Mamadou revealed.

"That's fine. This'll be the first time I've dined in a restaurant since the first time I was here, Mamadou, and you took Birdie and me to lunch near your downtown office. And then you took us out to dinner at the restaurant in Le Casino du Cap-Vert. Remember?"

"Yes, Mum Jane, I remember," he said with a smile.

We walked just a short distance. "Here we are. Walk up the stairs," he said as he opened the door to let all of us stream through in single file.

As soon as I got inside, it was evident that this was truly an upscale establishment. Even though it was the middle of the afternoon, there weren't any other patrons seated when we got there, so I got an unobstructed view of the entire dining room area. The floor had heavy, deep-pile carpeting. All of the tables were covered with cloth tablecloths. An attractive centerpiece adorned each table.

We were welcomed by two attendants working behind the bar which was located in the far corner of the room. We seated ourselves. No sooner were we seated when one of the attendants came over, welcomed us again, and distributed menus, saying, "When you are ready to order, I will be happy to serve you." We placed orders for beverages.

As soon as he came back with our beverages, the other attendant came over to take our orders for lunch. We all ordered the same thing—a shrimp entrée with Western-style French fries and salad.

It was quite a while before we were served, but my eyes lit up when I saw the server coming to our table with those huge shrimps piled up on our platters. As he set our platters before us, my thoughts went back to the dining room at Le Casino du Cap-Vert. I could hear the pianist playing Beethoven's *Moonlight Sonata* while we dined that night. I know now that it sounded corny, but I just couldn't resist sharing that as a highlight of the event.

Referring to the size of the shrimp, I explained, "In America, these shrimp would be called 'prawns,' which are the *crème de la crème* of crustaceans."

Directing my comment to Mamadou, I said, "I haven't seen shrimp this big since you took Birdie and me to dinner at Le Casino du Cap-Vert that night. Remember, Birdie ordered the shrimp dinner that night."

With a broad smile, he answered, "Yes, I remember, because I had a delicious steak dinner, and I especially remember that you ordered soup."

Directing this comment to the others, Mamadou recalled, "That was an extraordinary occasion, and I remember how happy Mum Jane was when the server brought her hot, steaming soup to the table and served her bowl from a big soup pot."

We made small talk during lunch and were cordially welcomed to come back by the restaurant staff as we left. We thanked them.

We walked back to the house where, as usual, family and friends were congregated in the living room. They were watching a television program. The dialogue was in Wolof.

A couple of days before, I had asked Mamadou's niece if she would plait my hair. So when I joined them in the living room, she asked me if this would be a good time for her to do it. Of course, I jumped at the chance.

So we went into the bedroom for privacy. It didn't take her but a very few minutes, and when she finished, I asked her what I should do to take care of it.

As she went through the motions, she told me, "Since your hair is very soft, tie a scarf around your head when you go to bed each night, and the plaits will last a long time."

I sat with the family for a while and then went out on the veranda to take some snapshots of the environs. While I was out there, Madame Gueye came out. I was surprised to see her, because I hadn't heard her when she came in. She asked me how I was enjoying myself. I told her about our late lunch at the new restaurant. She said she had heard about it when they had the grand opening.

While walking back into the living room to join the others, she told me she had come to take me to meet some more of her family members. I remembered that she had told me earlier that she wanted me to meet them before my naming ceremony.

In the presence of the others, she complimented my hairdo. I told her that Mamadou's niece had done it just a while before. The two of them exchanged a few words which I couldn't understand. I think their comments were in Wolof.

By then, it was near dark. Madame Gueye told me, "Come with me. I'm going to take you now before it gets too late."

We said good-bye and left the house. We rode a short distance through some dark streets. There were no street lights, so I couldn't tell where we were going, but it didn't make any difference, because I didn't know where we were, anyway. When she stopped the car, she told me to stay in the car until she came back, because she didn't know whether or not there was anybody at home. I sat there in the dark and waited for her.

When she came back, she told me to follow her. I got out and walked behind her as she led me into the house. There, I met some of her other family members, none of whom spoke any English. Among them was one of her aunts. Madame Gueye had told me that this was the aunt who was going to Mecca for the first time in her life. I figured out that Madame Gueye just wanted them to be able to say that they had met me before they came to my naming ceremony. Again, I appreciated the thought Madame Gueye had given to every detail.

When she had made all of the rounds of introduction, she drove us home. I was glad to get there, and soon afterward, I excused myself and went to my room. After making notes in my journal, I crawled into bed.

My Special Day

This was the special day for me—Jane Elizabeth Banks McIntosh.

Mamadou had told Madame Gueye to have me at his house at ten o'clock the next morning. The ceremony would take place in the parlor of his home.

As appropriate attire, I had brought my *bou-bou* that Mamadou's tailor had made for me to wear at his wedding. That's what I intended to wear for my naming ceremony.

I asked Madame Gueye, "Should I take my attire with me or should I put it on now?"

"Put it on now and wear it," she advised.

"OK, I'll do that," I acquiesced.

We sat down to our continental breakfast, and as soon as we finished, I dressed. Madame Gueye was already dressed.

We left the house in her car. Riding along, I soaked up the ambiance and character of the environs, admiring the natives in their colorful African garbs as they hustled and bustled through the streets to carry out their daily routines and business. I was trying desperately to keep my mind off the vague and ill-defined aspects of what this special event would turn out to be. I didn't know the procedure, what had been planned, or what I was supposed to do, if anything. Therefore, I had no idea what to expect.

All I knew was what Mamadou had told me—that the event had been scheduled and arranged just for me. Then and there, I would be given a Senegalese name at my naming ceremony.

All kinds of questions were twirling around in my head, *Would I say and do the right thing, or would I say and do the wrong thing? Would I meet their expectations, or would I disappoint them and not be given my Senegalese name?*

To slow down the whirling, I thought about Madame Gueye's next-door neighbor whom I had met just the day before. She had assured me that she'd attend the ceremony. From there, my thoughts immediately floated to Mamadou's countryman whom I had met at the JFK Air Afrique departure area. He too said he'd attend to witness my naming ceremony. My heart was swelling with so much pride, those thoughts almost brought tears to my eyes to think that those people had just met me, but they had bonded simply because of my relationship with Mamadou and Madame Gueye.

At that time, I had no conception of what future relationship the naming ceremony would build.

When we arrived, there were people already seated in the parlor. As soon as they acknowledged my presence, Madame Gueye said, "Jane, follow me."

I followed her. She led me into that large adjacent bedroom. Mamadou's sister came right behind me. I didn't know then, but later, I'd understand their attentiveness.

Madame Gueye said, "You must have a covering for your head." The two of them began draping my head with a long, wide scarf. It was made of a heavy material of dark, warm colors. The minute they put that scarf on my head, I began to sweat.

"Come with me," Madame Gueye ordered as she led me back into the parlor.

I followed her. Mamadou's sister followed right behind me as I was led to the center of the room where there was a large square mat.

Madame Gueye said, "Sit on the mat."

I could see that in the meantime, the room had filled with men, women, and children—some were seated on the sofas and chairs, and others were on folding chairs along the wall.

I cautiously sat down on the mat on the floor with my legs outstretched in front of me. Of course, I was barefoot, having taken off my shoes before entering the living room area.

I looked at the big round-faced clock on the wall directly in front of me. The time was 12:50 PM and I was reminded that Mamadou had told Madame Gueye to have me there by ten o'clock. But time didn't really mean anything to me at the moment, because all the while, I was thinking, *What are they going to do to me to give me my Senegalese name?* In fact, it had just dawned on me that I had never given this a second thought from the moment Mamadou asked me if I would like to have a naming ceremony at which time I'd be given my Senegalese name.

Draped and Seated for My Naming Ceremony

As I glanced around the room, I was comforted when I saw Mamadou and Suweeyah smiling at me. Among the sea of other faces, I recognized Mamadou's countryman whom I met at Air Afrique gate, Madame Gueye's next-door-neighbor, Madame Gueye's sisters, and Mamadou's sisters, mother, and niece. I recognized other faces among them, but I couldn't readily put names to their faces.

Just then, several elderly gentlemen entered the room. They all came in together. One of them went over and sat down beside Mamadou. Immediately, they began talking to each other.

Mamadou began translating by saying, "Mum Jane Elizabeth Banks McIntosh, the elder has come to begin the ceremony. This naming ceremony in your honor is being held for you by your Senegalese family here in Dakar, Senegal, West Africa. He is defining the ritual for two kinds of ceremonies."

After a short pause, Mamadou translated, "Mum Jane, he told me to ask you if you are Christian or Muslim."

Shocked, but without hesitation, I said, "I'm Christian."

The two of them exchanged a word or two, and then Mamadou said, "I told him you are Christian. He said that since you are Christian and are not being converted to Islam, the ceremony will be short and simple."

That statement caught me completely off guard and left me a bit unsettled, but I emphaticallly responded by saying, "Oh no, I'm not being converted to Islam."

The two of them exchanged a few words, and then Mamadou went right on translating and asked me, "Is your father living?"

I responded, "No, my father is deceased. Why are you asking?"

The two of them exchanged a few more words.

Mamadou translated what the elder stated. "Since your father is not living, you may select a male in the Senegalese family to name you."

I didn't know what to say, so I didn't say anything.

Mamadou said, "Mum Jane, just sit there."

Two of the elders, Madame Gueye, Mamadou, and Mamadou's sister went into seclusion in the adjacent bedroom.

The living room was silent. I rather fearfully guessed that they were consorting as to what to do about me. Cautiously, I looked around the room but sat perfectly still. I must admit, I was scared to death.

All the while, I was asking myself, *Did I do the right thing by accepting Mamadou's and Madame Gueye's honor of their holding a naming ceremony for me?*

In just a couple of minutes, they all came out. Mamadou and the elder took their seats. My confidence was restored when I saw Mamadou and Suweeyah smiling at me. I must admit that at that moment, the others were just a sea of faces. I couldn't identify anyone. I was confused, bewildered, and nervous. To be honest, I was frightened.

In his charismatic presence and authoritarian manner, Mamadou stood before me and announced, "On this day, February 19, 2001, you are given your Senegalese name. Your Senegalese name is Fatou Ndoye. My sister, Fatou, has given you her first name. Your last name is Ndoye. Madame Gueye has given you her maiden name, Ndoye. They have given you their names because by having their names, it will make you their sister."

Unwittingly, I impulsively asked, "What do the names mean?" After asking, I felt penitent, because as yet I hadn't been told whether or not to speak.

But without hesitation, Mamadou clearly enunciated, "Your first name, 'Fatou,' means 'caring sister.' Your last name, 'Ndoye,' means 'completeness.' Ndoye is a famous name in Senegal, and anywhere you go where people are familiar with African names, they will know the meaning of both of your names."

I felt relieved, and after a short pause, all I could think of was to say, "I am deeply honored. Thank you. Thank you."

"The ceremony is over," Mamadou responded.

I was numb with humility, excitement, and other mixed emotions I couldn't sort out. I tried to stand up, but couldn't after having been seated for such a long time in one position. Mamadou stepped over, took my arm, and helped me to get up from the mat.

Speaking and smiling all at the same time, they gathered around me with approving looks and hugs. Mamadou translated that they were all telling me how happy they were to welcome me as a member of their Senegalese family.

I expressed my gratitude to them for welcoming me into their family and told them I felt honored that so many family members and friends had come to be with me and witness this very special occasion.

Mamadou translated for them what I'd said as the group dispersed. All at the same time, a large straw mat was spread on the floor, a linen tablecloth was placed over the mat, and a large platter of food was placed in the center of the tablecloth. The group began singing and dancing.

Madame Gueye, Mamadou, and several family members gathered around the platter of beef, rice, and vegetables. I was given a spoon to eat with, but Mamadou, Madame Gueye, her sister, and the others ate in traditional Senegalese style.

Shortly after we ate, I told Madame Gueye that I wasn't feeling well and that I thought I'd better go home. I thanked everyone for coming. Madame Gueye and I said goodbye to everyone. Madame Gueye took my arm. We walked to the car. She drove me home.

I went to bed immediately because I was nauseous and felt violently ill. My instincts and my body organs were telling me that I had dyspepsia accompanied by dysentery.

Frequently during the night, I had to run back and forth to the bathroom. All the while, I was praying that my condition wouldn't require professional medical attention, so I just suffered the discomfort. My embarrassment was no less than my malady, because I was soiling my nightie and the bed linen.

Apparently, Madame Gueye became aware of my getting up and down all through the night. Finally, she came into my room and saw my predicament. She promptly aroused her house helpers. They came in and stripped my bed while I changed into a clean nightie.

She called me out of the bedroom and ordered me to sit at the table in the foyer. She set a bowl of white stuff before me. It was steaming hot. It looked like some kind of porridge.

I was repulsed by the sight of it and the thought of putting anything into my stomach made it gurgle.

I asked her, "What is this?"

She replied, "It is hot rice soup."

I took a sip of it. It was salty but I couldn't taste any other seasoning in it. Not wanting to hurt her feelings, I told her, "That doesn't taste good to me right now. I'll drink it later."

She ordered me, "Drink it now. It will be good for you."

In another receptacle, she brought me some sweet hot cinnamon-tasting tea. I took one sip. "Oh, that tastes good, and it feels good going down," I said as I drank all of it.

She left the room for a moment, and when she came back, she looked in my rice soup bowl and saw that I hadn't touched it since she left.

"You must drink the rice soup. It is good for your problem, and it will make you feel better," she said in a firm, motherly tone of voice.

I wanted to hold my nose, but I managed to sip most of it.

By that time, her house helpers had changed my bed, so I retired to my room, laid my weakened body down, and finally went to sleep.

The Day After

By the time I awoke the next morning, Mamadou, Suweeyah, and Mamadou's brother were there to visit me. They didn't know it, but I really didn't feel up to socializing. However, I quelled my feelings as best I could.

When I joined them in the foyer, they excitedly announced, "Madame Gueye will be in Washington, DC in March. While she's in the country, she'll be coming to visit us for three days in Maple Heights, Ohio."

Suweeyah added, "Mum Jane, it would really be nice if you could come and be with us while she's there."

"I'll let you know when I get back home, because it'll all depend on my husband's condition at that time," I told them in no uncertain terms.

Madame Gueye was discreet and told them in Wolof that I had a medical problem during the night. They appeared surprised but understanding. Soon they all left.

She told me to come with her because she was going to take me to the pharmacy to get some medicine. She and I went out the door.

We walked in the same direction as the charcoal manufacturer's workshop. Oddly enough, I was feeling much better by the time we got to the pharmacy. There, we were greeted by a tall regal-looking African woman. Madame Gueye introduced the woman as her friend, the pharmacist and owner.

I was thoroughly impressed because she spoke clear English when she acknowledged the introduction. All at the same time, I noticed that she had two assistants in the store with her. The store was clean, and the shelves were stocked meticulously.

I told her about my problem. She stepped away momentarily, scanned an over-the-counter shelf of medicines, picked up a box and brought it to me.

Directing her advice to both Madame Gueye and me, she carefully explained, "This is a box of fourteen two-hundred-milligram capsules of nifuroxazide. Take

138

one immediately, but do not exceed three more during the next twenty-four-hour period."

She emphatically advised Madame Gueye, "If her condition does not subside within a twenty-four-hour period, let me know, and I will refer you to a physician to whom you can take her for treatment. However, this medication should take effect immediately and fortify her against another attack."

Madame Gueye paid for the medication, chatted with her for a moment, and then told the pharmacist she wanted to get me back to her home right away so I could take the medicine.

I thanked the pharmacist for her professional assistance as we left. On the way out the door, Madame Gueye said, "The patisserie is close, so I'm going to get you a fresh-baked baguette of French bread before we go back to the house."

When we got home, Madame Gueye gave me a dose of the medicine and said, "You look tired. I think you should lie down."

I went to my room. I immediately noticed that my extra set of bed linens and nightie had been washed, dried, folded, and placed on the other twin bed. I stretched out on my bed. I must have fallen asleep.

When I awakened, there was a big difference in the way I felt. The house was quiet, but I walked out to the living room where Madame Gueye was relaxing on the sofa. She was reading while nibbling from a tray of cheese and French bread. She welcomed me to join her for some nibbles.

She sat up and said in a concerned tone of voice, "How are you feeling now?"

"Oh, I'm feeling a lot better," I was happy to tell her. As I did so, I helped myself to the cheese and bread. "Oh, this really tastes good. This is the first solid food I've had in my stomach since yesterday, and I lost all of that during the night."

I sat with her for a little while longer, fascinated as I watched her house helpers busy themselves with their household chores. One of them was watering and tending the shrubs while the other one scrubbed the marble entrance next to the front door. As I watched, I wondered what Madame Gueye did around the house.

I helped myself to some more of the cheeses left on the platter. In Wolof, she called out to someone. Promptly, one of her house helpers brought me a chilled glass and a bottle of water.

In her motherly manner, Madame Gueye came over to me, opened a bottle of water, poured it into the glass, and said, "Drink some of this water. I think you need some fluids."

She went back to her reading. I went to my room and picked up my journal. On the way back, I stopped off and sat down at the table to make some notes in the sun room next to the indoor/outdoor garden.

To my surprise, one of her house helpers came over to me. She spoke no English, so she said nothing. She just extended her arms. As I got up to embrace her, she put her arm around my shoulder, smiled and looked me straight in the eye. I think she was demonstrating her sympathy for what I'd gone through during the night.

I made a valiant attempt through my facial expressions and by my embrace, to express my appreciation for what they'd done to lessen my pain of embarrassment.

I went back to making notes in my journal. When I finished, I told Madame Gueye that I'd forego any suggestion of further activity that day. I then excused myself and went back to my room. I still felt a little sick and weak, and my stomach was still not completely settled. So I took another dose of the medicine and drank some more water. Soon after I lay down, I fell asleep.

My Encounter at the Embassy

When I awoke, I felt almost back to normal. As we were having our continental breakfast, Mamadou and Suweeyah came in.

It was apparent that they were concerned about me, but I was happy to be able to tell them how much better I was after having taken the medicine from the pharmacist.

After we talked for a while, it came up in conversation that I needed to go to the American Embassy and get the necessary information and forms to complete so I could begin the process of applying for the work visa for Mamadou's niece. While my enthusiasm was high, I asked if we could go then. Of course, Mamadou obliged, got a taxi and took me there.

We all got out of the taxi and walked the short distance to the front of the building. I walked up to the receptionist's window. I stood there for about five minutes before the clerk eventually acknowledged my presence at the window.

When she did finally acknowledge my presence, I stated my name and showed her my passport. After she examined it and handed it back to me, I explained my purpose for being there.

She asked me what I considered to be idiotic questions, and so I became defensive. She related to me in a negative, curt, suspicious, and hostile manner. Therefore, I took advantage of the opportunity to advise and remind her that I was a native-born, tax-paying United States citizen. I then demanded that she just discharge her clerical duty and give me all of the necessary forms to complete in order to apply for a work visa.

After our verbal confrontation, the rigidity in her countenance fell. She acquiesced, complied with my request, and gave me what I asked for. As she handed the forms to me, I took great pleasure in repeating that I was a tax-paying American citizen. From the expression on her face, I felt assured that she absorbed the full intent of my reiteration.

My first, and probably my last experience at the US Embassy in Dakar, Senegal was enlightening, but infuriating.

As we left the building, we decided to go to some boutiques and do some shopping.

We got another taxi. The driver took us where Mamadou directed him. Before we got out, Mamadou told me that I needed to be vigilant because parts of that area weren't considered as safe as others. He demanded, "You are not to leave my side, and give me your purse."

I obeyed with no hesitation and trotted along beside him like a little girl.

After going into several other boutiques along the way, I concluded that I wasn't going to find the design of the garment I had in mind, so Mamadou suggested that we go to his tailor's shop. We caught another taxi.

When we walked in, the tailor was busy at his sewing machine. He stopped sewing, came to the counter, and greeted us. Mamadou introduced me to him. To my surprise, he acknowledged the introduction in English. He and Mamadou held a brief conversation for a minute or so during which Mamadou stated our purpose for being there. He then directed the conversation to me. I told the tailor what I'd been looking for but hadn't found anything close to it. While I was telling him, I tore a sheet of paper from my journal and made a sketch of the garment I was looking for. I showed the sketch to him and asked him if he could make two garments with the same design and have them ready for me before I left to go back to America. He assured me that he could. He took me into his fabric inventory room where there were hundreds of bolts of fabric. I picked out the material. He took my measurements and quoted his price. I accepted his quote. He told Mamadou he'd have them ready and when to bring me back to pick them up.

I expressed my thanks and that it was my pleasure to have met him. With that accomplished, we left to get another taxi. We went back to Mamadou's house. We spent the rest of the day relaxing with family and friends after a light repast of prawns, green salad, French bread and Fanta sodas. That really tasted good, because my appetite had returned to normal.

Mamadou asked me if I felt up to taking a trip to a village the next day. He told me he'd like for me to visit the village where his spiritual leader lived. I forgot all about how I felt and didn't hesitate for one moment about going. In fact, I was overjoyed by the opportunity to visit another village in West Africa.

Immediately, he and his niece began making plans. They agreed that it wouldn't be prudent for all of us to stay overnight in the village, so we'd leave early the next morning, spend the day there, and then return to Dakar the same night. With those plans in the making, Mamadou got a taxi and took me home to Madame Gueye's.

When I got there, I told her of our plans.

Quizzingly, she asked, "Do you feel like going?"

"Oh yes, I'm fine now," I assured her. "Are you free to go with us?"

She declined.

Shortly, I took a shower, went to my room, set my alarm clock and went to bed since they told me we would leave the next morning at eight o'clock.

My Trip to the Village of Santhiousine and My Interview with Mamadou's Spiritual Leader

The next morning, I was awakened by a familiar soft knock on my door. Madame Gueye said softly that Mamadou's brother had come to pick me up to take me to Mamadou's house from where we were to leave to go to the village. While I was dressing, I kept thinking, *I know I set my travel alarm clock, so what happened that it didn't go off?* Then it dawned on me that I'd been a bit under the weather and not yet quite back to normal. I dismissed that from my mind and focused on what was ahead for me that day, another day in my Motherland.

I hurriedly ate my continental breakfast. Madame Gueye gave us her good wishes for a rewarding experience, and in just a few minutes, we left her house.

We traveled through the marketplaces and onto the main street. A section of the road was closed, so we had to detour. The road was bumpy, but soon we were back on smooth pavement of the main street that led to Mamadou's house.

Everybody was ready. Two drivers were waiting for us and we all loaded up in the two cars that were parked there. As we got in, Mamadou announced that we'd be making a brief stop at the supermarket to pick up a few things before we launched on our journey to the village. We pulled away from his house, and surely enough, not far from there, we stopped at a supermarket.

That highway was smooth until we came to an unanticipated stop for gas. While the cars were being gassed up, everybody got out and went into the convenience store to get cold drinks to take with us as we rode.

Along our way, we passed a forest. In true tour-guide persona, Mamadou said as he pointed, "We are passing by a baobab tree forest. The baobab tree is native to Africa. It is called 'the tree of life' because every part of the tree provides some entity of life to some creature for sustenance."

In a clearing near that narrow road, I noticed a young boy and a dog. The boy was chasing rabbits. That was a reminder to me that he might have been hunting rabbits for sale or to put meat on his family's table.

Near some railroad tracks that ran east and west, we passed a sheep farm. But for the most part, the scenery was dense vegetation and tall stately trees. The branches were slightly waving in the hot breeze.

We didn't stop any more and just before we turned off onto the road leading into the village, we slowed to a snail's pace. The roadbed was soft. I could see and feel that we were riding on loose sand. There was no mistake that we were definitely "in the bush."

We had arrived at the village where Mamadou's spiritual leader lived. I lost track of everybody else, because Mamadou said to me, "Mum Jane, come with me. I want to take you to talk with my spiritual leader."

I felt almost reverent but followed him. Slowly, he led me in the direction of a structure that looked like a hut not far from where our driver had parked the car. The closer I got to the structure, the more it looked like just that—a hut.

Spiritual Leader's Hut

When we got there, just outside an opening, Mamadou said, "Wait right here, Mum Jane." He slipped out of his shoes and walked through the opening.

I stood perfectly still but looked in. There sat a very distinguished-looking elderly gentleman. (His discourse was being delivered in a commanding tone of voice. It sounded as if we had arrived in the middle of a lecture.)

I wondered, *Is that man Mamadou's spiritual leader?*

He was seated facing a group of six or eight young men ranging in age from about nine to twelve. The spiritual leader had their undivided attention, because their eyes were fixed on his face. They appeared to be listening intently to everything he was telling them, and the atmosphere in the hut was that of a classroom.

Immediately, I was impressed and observed that none of the boys were distracted when Mamadou walked in. (To me that was a stark contrast between their demeanor and some boys who tend to be easily distracted in our public school classrooms in America.)

During the monologue, Mamadou walked over to an area behind his spiritual leader. He picked up a pillow and walked over to the open space behind the group of young men facing the spiritual leader. He placed the pillow on the ground, and motioned for me to come in and sit on the pillow. I followed his directions.

Wow! It was dreadfully hot in there. I saw another opening on the opposite side from where we entered the hut, but there was no breeze blowing through either of the two openings.

Soon after I sat down, I opened my portfolio and began making some notes in my journal.

As I looked around, I observed that the hut was just one large enclosure. The sides were made of heavy corrugated plastic similar to what I've seen used in America for an inexpensive patio cover. The supporting beams looked like large tree trunks. The enclosure was sparsely furnished with a chiffonier and two beds. Mamadou translated later that one bed was for the spiritual leader. However, he was a very humble person and preferred to sleep on the floor. The other bed was for a sick person under treatment from him.

Just then two young men appeared at the opening. I think they were late for class. They slipped out of their flip-flops, left them outside, and then knelt and crawled to join the group seated on the mat in front of the spiritual leader.

Shortly, a lady appeared in the opening. Slowly, she walked in. She and the spiritual leader exchanged a few words, and then she left.

The Spiritual Leader continued his discourse.

While he was lecturing, I made a note in my journal that he was holding some large, brown object in his hand and all at the same time, he was peeling it.

In a little while, the lady came back. This time, she was accompanied by another lady. The three of them spoke very briefly. The spiritual leader wrote something on a piece of paper and wrapped the paper around something that looked like powdered herbs. He handed the package to one of them. Then the two ladies left.

The spiritual leader said something to the boys. They stood up and quietly left the hut.

It was then that Mamadou told me that his spiritual leader had dismissed the class early but that I could stay.

Mamadou, his spiritual leader, and I were alone in that hut. Mamadou re-introduced me to his spiritual leader as Fatou Ndoye. It caught me by surprise when Mamadou said he had told the spiritual leader that I'd like to talk with him. The two of us had not discussed that.

Immediately, it flashed through my mind, *Oh, this surely will be a highlight of my visit to the village of Santhiousine.*

Mamadou translated our conversation back and forth. We both acknowledged that I had attended Mamadou's wedding. Without any delay in lapse of time, Mamadou translated to me that his spiritual leader told him to inform me, "It is not a common practice for a woman to be in my hut. But I have made an exception for you, because you are Mamadou's *sama yaye*, a new member of the Senegalese family, and a special guest from America."

At that point, there was no doubt in my mind that Mamadou had told his spiritual leader of my naming ceremony and how meaningful it was for them to welcome me into their family.

His spiritual leader told me, "Fatou, I welcome you into your Senegalese family!"

Mamadou enlightened me by explaining, "Because of our relationship, he has invited you to come inside and talk with him. But generally, women sit outside his hut and extend greetings, and he prays for them."

I didn't know what to say, except, "I thank you for welcoming me. Already, I feel bonded with my family. And thank you for honoring me in such a special way. I feel revered beyond description."

Mamadou translated my response to his welcoming words.

We smiled at one another, and after a brief pause, he picked up the object he had been peeling while lecturing his class.

To initiate dialogue, I asked him, "What is that you're peeling?"

"It is a kola nut," he answered. "It was originally native to central Africa, but it is now cultivated in a number of other tropical countries."

Because I'd seen him hand that lady some herbs, my next question was, "Do you have healing powers?"

Unequivocally, he answered, "Yes, I have a special gift for healing."

Just then, a gentleman appeared at a side opening in the hut. He walked inside. He and the spiritual leader spoke briefly. He handed the man the peeled kola nut. The man turned and walked out through the opening.

"Do you live here?" I asked.

Looking me straight in the eye, Mamadou translated his answer, saying, "Yes, I live here. This is my home. I do not want to live anywhere else. This is my village—the village of Santhiousine."

As Mamadou went on translating, he told me that his spiritual leader's village was a community where men and women did not live in the same section. He said that the men lived together in the front section; the women lived together in the back section.

"Is this village inhabited by an ethnic group?" I asked.

He answered, "Yes, this village is inhabited by an ethnic group, but the population is not entirely Wolof."

"Approximately how many people live here?" I asked.

"About fifteen hundred people live here," he replied.

All of a sudden, Mamadou interjected and called our attention to more visitors who had come in from Dakar after we arrived. I could hear voices of several other people as they walked a short distance from the opening on the side of the hut.

I asked Mamadou, "How did they get here?"

He answered, "To get here, one must take public transportation from Dakar and then travel by automobile to the village, just as we did."

His spiritual leader went on to tell me that his village was around a hundred years old. He said that the history of the village was told to each generation, because it affected their way of life. Therefore, their history perpetuated their culture and lifestyle.

Mamadou translated that I said, "I can't resist suggesting that your history should be recorded, since it is so significant as a part of your African heritage."

He agreed as he went on to tell me that when we came in, he was just finishing a lesson with a class of his students.

I thought it to be an appropriate moment to tell him that I was a retired instrumental music public school teacher. So I asked him, "What subjects do you teach?"

In answer to that question, Mamadou translated that they learned the holy book and how to read and write Arabic. They learned science, agriculture, academics, wisdom, high moral conduct, good judgment, sharing, pride, and obedience.

He placed emphasis on obedience and said, "Obedience is a mandate and is stressed in my classes. Students are cautioned that disobedience could precipitate something dreadful happening to them in their lives."

The spiritual leader said that all of the academic subjects and virtues he taught were required in order to launch a career, become successful, and lead a moral life. Consequently, many of his students went out to set up their own businesses. Of course, some of them remain in the village and acquire land to cultivate.

At this point, I shared with him that I was impressed as I observed his students' attentiveness while he was teaching them. "I noticed that your students are all boys. There were no girls among them. Who is responsible for teaching and nurturing the girls?"

Unhesitatingly, he answered, "The women."

He told me that the village children were taught by their parents, the spiritual leader, and his disciples. They did not go to school outside the village. Their classes began early in the morning; their afternoons were free.

As I wiped a river of sweat running down from my head onto my face, the thought ran through my mind, *It would be inhumane to hold classes in the afternoon, because it's unbearably hot in this hut—and this only February. What is it like during the summer months?*

I put that thought out of my mind and asked him, "Do you charge for your lessons?"

"No, I do not charge for lessons, but I will accept money," he answered.

He went on to say that many "so-called" spiritual leaders had come to the area but that some of them were imposters. Those who were imposters tried to deceive the villagers by charging fees, sometimes in covert ways. He said that some of them even tried to convert the villagers to Christian religion.

I wondered if he was referring to missionaries from America. But to be honest, I was reluctant, even afraid, to ask.

"Has your village ever been invaded?" I asked.

"Oh, no, never. That would be unheard of. The presence of God in this village precludes that as even a remote possibility," he answered confidently.

My impression of him reminded me of the chief in the village of Juffure and the chief in the village of Brufut Marimma, The Gambia. As a result, I was prompted to ask, "Are you called upon by the villagers for guidance and counseling?"

Mamadou translated his response to be, "As a spiritual leader, yes, I am consulted on spiritual, financial, personal, marital, and all kinds of matters."

At this point, he brought out the point that the entire village belonged to him. He said that the villagers had parcels of land on which they cultivated and harvested their own vegetables and then sold their own products. He told me that he had a plot of land that was cultivated just for him, but that some people gave him sugar and rice.

He pointed out that since his village was such a long way from the ocean, they weren't able to get fish, so their principal meats were lamb and chicken which they raised right there in the village.

Just then, the spiritual leader's chief disciple came in with three young men, I would say about nine years old. They were all barefoot. They were carrying three plastic cups. Following right behind them, Mamadou's brother came in. He was carrying three bottles of water. He handed each of us a bottle of water, and the boys handed us a cup. The sight of water was most welcome. I hadn't realized it until I saw the water, but my mouth was actually parched.

The chief disciple said something to the boys. All together, they left through that same opening. Just outside, they slipped into their flip-flops that they had left just outside before they came in. One by one, they disappeared from sight. I could only surmise that the disciple had told the boys that the spiritual leader was being interviewed by Mamadou's guest from America.

Through an opening on the other side of the hut, I saw a child who was slipping out of its flip-flops. I couldn't really tell whether it was a boy or girl. I think it was a boy, but the child looked to be a three-and-a-half to four-year-old. He came in, walked up to the spiritual leader, and said something to him. The spiritual leader responded in a soft, gentle tone of voice. The child backed up to the opening, turned around, gave the spiritual leader a short eye-to-eye stare, went out, and disappeared from the opening. I was awestruck. That fascinated me.

Interviewing Mamadou's Spiritual Leader

Almost as if he were reading my mind because I was just about to open the subject, he resumed our conversation by telling me, "The people in my village are not poor. The people in my village do not want to modernize with electricity, plumbing, water purification, and other urban conveniences. Instead, they want to hold on to their traditions."

I had been perplexed as to how I was going to approach that subject, but he volunteered the information without my having to wrestle with a question that wouldn't sound condescending or demeaning.

He went on to say that many villagers, and even some with children, had left their homes in the village and gone to the city, anticipating a modern lifestyle, only to find, unfortunately, that there was no work for them. He looked and sounded sad as he told me that many of them ended up "homeless."

It was a welcome sight when Mamadou's niece appeared at the opening of the hut. It was conspicuous that she couldn't enter his hut. She merely announced to Mamadou and me that she had cooked a meal for us and that it was ready. Nobody would ever know how good that sounded to me, because all I had eaten that day was a continental breakfast just before I left Madame Gueye's house in Dakar.

As I got up, I told him, "Thank you so very much for talking with me. It's been a privilege, and I consider it an honor that I will cherish forever."

He smiled at me, and Mamadou translated that he said, "Welcome to your Motherland and your Senegalese family."

I wanted to shake his hand, but restrained myself, not knowing whether it was proper or appropriate for his culture and also since he was a man of such high esteem.

He and Mamadou exchanged a word or two as we said good-bye to him. Mamadou and I walked out through the opening of the hut. I followed behind him as he led me to a large house situated not far from the spiritual leader's hut.

When we walked into the house, I marveled at the sight of bales of rice stacked one on top of the other along the wall of one room.

The meal Mamadou's niece had prepared for us consisted of two separate meats—chicken for Suweeyah and herself and beef for the rest of us—ready to be served when we arrived. We had rice, vegetables, and French bread and butter with the meats.

Although it was almost too hot to eat, that didn't deter me, because by then, I was famished. When we were all served, I noticed that the men went to one section of the house and we women went to another.

Men Dining Alone

When we finished eating, we went outside. The sun had gone down a bit, but it was still hot. Mamadou volunteered to lead us on a tour of the village. Everyone in our group followed as Mamadou led us. Most of the villagers appeared to know him, and there was no doubt in my mind that he was familiar with the layout of the village.

It warmed my heart as the little children followed us everywhere we went. Along the way, I took pictures of them. I could tell that they liked having their pictures taken because they posed for each one. At the end of the tour, they all lined up and we passed out treats to them.

By that time, it was just before sundown. We said good-bye to everybody and loaded up in our cars to head back to town.

We got only a few yards from the compound when, of all things, the car got stuck in that loose sand we had so uneventfully navigated when riding into the village. Our driver tried and tried, but he couldn't get enough traction to move the car an inch forward or backward. He even tried to steer the car to the side of the path, but he still couldn't get traction. I wondered how he was ever going to maneuver through that sand so we could get to the highway that would take us back to Dakar.

Pessimistic about our quandary, I imagined having to spend the night in that hot car. All the while, the driver was revving the motor so hard, I even feared that we'd run out of gas way out there.

After many unsuccessful attempts, our dilemma drew attention from some of the men villagers. So, several men came to our rescue and pushed the car until the driver got traction out of the sand.

Hooray! We were back on solid ground, headed for the highway!

Since it was daylight and I was so excited when we rode into the village, I hadn't noticed the condition of the road or the driver's pattern, but as soon as he drove onto the highway, I could see that it was just one lane in each direction, and the dividing line was barely visible.

And, to my dismay, I saw the driver take several unnecessary chances. That compounded my feeling that we were traveling at an excessive speed. From then on, I relentlessly watched the road and his driving pattern.

As we sped along, of course we were met by oncoming cars headed in the opposite direction. I noticed that some of the cars had only one headlight, and some headlights were so dim, I could barely see them. To make matters worse, many of the drivers were not exercising customary road courtesy. They were honking their horns at each other and driving erratically. In my judgment, all of them were driving too fast for road conditions.

I took it as long as I could, and then I peeked over our driver's shoulder to look at the speedometer. It read one hundred miles per hour. I nearly panicked.

The driver spoke no English, and of course, I couldn't speak his language or I would have told him myself. So I told Mamadou to tell the driver that he was going too fast.

In a very diplomatic tone of voice, Mamadou said something to him in Wolof. I had no doubt that he conveyed my concern to the driver, because I could feel the driver reduce his speed for a few miles.

Then, intuitively, I could feel that he had picked up his speed. Again, I peeked over his shoulder and saw that he was back up at one hundred miles per hour.

I spoke about it to Mamadou again, but more emphatically. In the words of reprimand, I told him that at the speed of one hundred miles per hour in that raggedy car, at no time were all four wheels down on the pavement, and that was not safe. I demanded that he slow down.

In a more forceful tone of voice, Mamadou said something to the driver again. I was sure he conveyed my anxiety to the driver, because he reduced his speed.

All at the same time, I could see that we were overtaking a large object up ahead of us. It looked like the back of a trailer. Since there were no taillights on the object, for a second or two I thought I was having an optical illusion. The closer we got to the object, the more sure I was that it wasn't an illusion, because we had caught up with it.

Just in the nick of time, our driver put on his brakes. We had just avoided a rear-end crash into the back of a semitrailer!

I was panic-stricken. I reprimanded Mamadou by saying, "You see, when you're driving at such a high speed, no driver has sufficient time to react appropriately in the event of an unforeseen circumstance such as what we just encountered."

As emphatically as I could, I told Mamadou, "You tell that driver that I said for him to go slower and drive at a safe speed."

Mamadou spoke up and conveyed my message in a very emphatic tone of voice. That was enough for the driver to heed my reprimand, because he cautiously passed the trailer truck and drove at a sensible speed for the rest of the trip back to Dakar.

There was little conversation for the rest of the journey until Mamadou broke the silence. He said, "Mum Jane, give me your return itinerary, and I will call to confirm your reservation for your departure."

I told him I would give it to him when we got back to Madame Gueye's house. I thought no more about it because of his experience in the travel industry.

Finally, we rolled into Dakar. The driver took me to Madame Gueye's house. I breathed a deep sigh of relief and thanked God for His care.

As soon as I got there, I went to my room, pulled out my travel reservations and handed the information and ticket to Mamadou. He said he would call the airline the next day to ensure that my travel plans were in place. With that, he bade us good night and left to get back into the taxi.

I gave Madame Gueye and her husband a cursory account of my day's adventure and activity, emphasizing my privileged interview with Mamadou's spiritual leader in his hut. I de-emphasized our getting stuck in the sand and our near-miss accident on the terrifying ride back from the village.

They listened and smiled. Then she reminded me that she had promised to take me to shop in some boutiques the next day. She assured me that I'd surely find some authentic African fashions to take back home for my wardrobe.

I took a shower and got ready for bed.

I thanked God for keeping me safe so I could get back home to Gaines. I sat on the side of my bed and made copious notes before I crawled in.

Preparation for Departure

Upon arising, I began to seriously and systematically pack for departure the next day. That was unlike me, because when packing to go home, I literally "throw" my things in my luggage. This time, I packed meticulously so as to leave enough room to pack my tailor-made garments and any boutique garments I might purchase later that day to take home with me.

Then I joined Madame Gueye for our continental breakfast. As soon as we finished, we took off to go shopping. She told me that we'd take a taxi because we'd be going to several places. I agreed with her judgment. We walked a block or two. She hailed a taxi, and we were on our way.

While we were riding, she advised that for my own safety, I should let her carry my money. I gave her my wallet for safekeeping.

When we arrived at an emporium, we got out and browsed around. I selected some souvenir bracelets and various and sundry other items to take home for family and friends. She bartered with the merchants and paid them from my wallet. When I finished browsing, she hailed another taxi. We went to three other boutiques. I didn't find anything that caught my fancy, so from there she hailed another taxi and took me to yet another shop located a few blocks away.

The merchants there also greeted her as if she were a celebrity. Again, I realized that she must have been a valued customer. I fell for two beautiful outfits—one was a *bou-bou* and the other was a *dokcat*. I tried them on. They both fit me perfectly. I then selected an outfit for Gaines. Madame Gueye negotiated the price for all of my selections and paid the merchant from my wallet. She exchanged cordialities with them, and then we left.

I told Madame Gueye that I didn't anticipate any more purchases, and so I needed to convert my Senegalese CFAs back into US currency except for enough CFAs to pay the tailor for the garments he was making for me.

She suggested that we go to the bank while we were out. We hopped into another taxi but when we got to the bank, we discovered a sign on the door. In English, the sign read "Bank Closed from 1300 hours to 1600 hours."

We left the bank and took a taxi back to her home. Soon after we arrived, Mamadou came in. He told us he had called a short time before to let me know that he checked with Air Afrique to confirm my itinerary. He said he was informed that I had no reservation.

In the meantime, he said I should go with him to the tailor shop to pick up my garments and then he would take me to Air Afrique to clarify my flight status.

Madame Gueye explained to him that when she had taken me to the bank to exchange my currency, the bank was closed.

He looked at his watch and said, "No problem. I will see that she gets her currency exchanged." So off we went.

The first place we went was to the tailor shop. We were there just long enough for me to pick up my garments and pay the tailor. He thanked me for my business and said he hoped he would be able to do some work for me again.

We left there and went downtown to the Air Afrique ticket office. As we entered, a conspicuously posted sign directed us to "Take a Number." According to the timer on the wall, customer number 587 was being served. We took a number. My number was 600. We got in line to wait for my number to come up. We stood there and waited and waited. But the number on the timer on the wall never changed from 587.

Finally, a Senegalese man at one of the Air Afrique counters beckoned Mamadou to come to his counter. It was obvious to me that he recognized Mamadou standing in line. Mamadou took me by the hand and led me to the counter. They exchanged cordialities and then he told the agent that he had been told over the phone that there was no reservation for his *sama yaye*. He presented my itinerary and tickets. After a quick check on his computer, the agent confirmed my flight status and seat number as 15K. With that assurance, we left the ticket office.

From there, we went to what he called, the "white market" to convert my CFAs to U.S. dollars. That marketer wanted an exorbitant conversion fee. I told Mamadou, "Forget him."

We went a few doors down to another converter where Mamadou was able to get a reasonable conversion fee.

With all my errands completed, we went to Mamadou's house where his niece rebraided my hair. I thanked her and told her that she finally got the plaiting loose enough. Shortly, we were served a light meal of thinly sliced meats, cheese, French bread, and Fanta sodas.

After a while, Mamadou, Suweeyah, Mamadou's brother, their niece, and I took a cab to Madame Gueye's house. When we got there, Madame Gueye was out. While we were waiting for her to return, we talked about my visit to the American embassy. I assured Mamadou's niece that I had looked over the forms and pertinent information and would be working diligently to process her papers for a work visa for her to come to Hayward.

Madame Gueye came in shortly. She was carrying some shopping bags. Soon dinner was served. Her house helpers went through their ritual of spreading the straw mat and damask table cloth on the floor. We all sat down to a delicious meal.

After such a long, full day, we all said good night. Mamadou, Suweeyah, and Mamadou's niece promised to be at Madame Gueye's house early the next morning to go to the airport to see me off.

Madame Gueye told me to be up at seven o'clock in the morning and ready to leave for the airport for check-in time at 8:30.

I went to my room to finish packing, took a shower, made copious notes in my journal and then went to sleep.

Back to America

The folks were up long before seven o'clock, because I could hear them stirring around. So when I emerged from my room, the continental breakfast was on the table.

During breakfast, Mamadou and his family arrived. Mamadou put my luggage in Madame Gueye's car. She and I rode alone. Mamadou and his family followed us in their car. While we rode, I tried to express my gratitude to her for again honoring me as her special guest in their home. At the same time, I most sincerely extended another cordial open invitation to her and any member of her family to be guests of the McIntoshes if and when they were in America and could share some time with us in our home in Hayward, California. She again told me how much she cherished her visit to our home a few years before.

After we arrived at the airport, I knew we had to part, and it was truly bittersweet for me while we were saying our good-byes and assurances that we'd all continue to keep in close touch with one another. While I was saddened about leaving my family in Senegal, I was getting excited about going home, because I'd been àway from Gaines and my family in America for such a long time.

As they all sent their very best wishes to my family in America, I instinctively asked God to embrace and protect me during my journey home and at the same time to spare and bless me to return some day to revisit my Senegalese family.

Since none of them were ticketed, they all walked with me as far as they could. When I got to the passageway and presented my documents, I was informed that my flight had been delayed until 1400 hours. They all heard the agent's announcement. At that moment, it became my gut feeling that they all were aware of some of the problems that Air Afrique was experiencing during that time. However, none of them voiced any comment.

Instead, Madame Gueye spoke up and said, "Jane, I'll take you back to my house and we'll return in time for the 1400 hour flight."

I was at her mercy, so I accepted her accommodating me during this crisis. "I don't know how to thank you for your kindness," I said to her as we walked to the car.

While we were walking, Mamadou suggested, "We'll come back and meet you here just before your flight time."

Realizing that they had the day ahead of them, I insisted that they need not interrupt their plans just to accommodate Air Afrique. So, I felt duty bound to tell them, "Don't ruin your day. Go ahead with whatever you have planned."

Madame Gueye agreed and promised them that she would see to it that I got to the airport to catch the delayed flight.

With that, we said goodbye again. They left to go to their car.

Madame Gueye and I returned to her house. She went to her room, changed clothes, and when she came out, she said to me, "I must go to the market, and I want you to go with me."

She said something to one of her house helpers, because her house helper got into the back seat of the car just before we left the house.

At the market, she and the merchants greeted each other in their own familiar ways. She shopped for fish, vegetables, and French bread. I noticed that when each merchant handed Madame Gueye's purchases to her, she immediately handed the bags to her house helper. We didn't stay out very long or shop anywhere else.

We immediately returned to her house. Her house helper disappeared and went directly to the kitchen. I took off my shoes and joined Madame Gueye in the living room. But it wasn't long before I smelled onions, celery, and bell peppers being sautéed. I knew right away that her house helpers were preparing a meal for us.

She and I were in the middle of conversation. The doorbell rang. When she answered, to my surprise, Mamadou and his family walked in. As we greeted each other, they took off their shoes. She ushered them into the living room. They seated themselves. She left us in the living room.

"We came back to see you off again," Mamadou said in a rather whimsical tone of voice.

My heart was warmed by his saying that, and tears welled up in my eyes. Soon Madame Gueye and her house helpers came into the living room. They were carrying a tray of cold beverages and munchies. They set the tray on the coffee table. She took a seat in one of the big, overstuffed chairs. Her house helpers left the room. She told us to help ourselves to whatever we wanted to munch on while our meal was being prepared. We all helped ourselves.

As we munched, the conversation segued to Air Afrique and rumors of problems the airline was experiencing. They were judicious in their comments, but I got the impression that my plight was not uncommon during that particular time. My suspicions were right. They were aware that based on recent incidences and poor quality of service, the airline would soon cease operation.

While we were all together, I bemoaned my personal circumstances and shared my feelings of anxiety in relation to resuming my responsibilities at home. I told them that I was particularly concerned because of my commitment to caring for Gaines. They listened and tried to allay my fears in spite of what had happened.

Soon the house helpers went through their ritual of setting up for our meal. We gathered around the platter and enjoyed our last meal together just before we all departed to take me back to the airport.

When we got there, we said our good-byes again as they walked me to the passageway to enter the terminal. It appeared that procedures were in order. As they were not ticketed, it was customary for them to retreat from the restricted area. I proceeded through the passageway to go into the terminal. I turned around and waved to them as they stood in a group, waving their last good-byes to me.

I got in line to get my documents processed to go through customs and immigration. The departure gate area was hot and stuffy. There were hundreds of passengers milling around. I got in line. I could see that the line was not only unbelievably long, but also it wasn't moving. I stepped out of line, walked up to the gate agent and asked why the line wasn't moving. The agent informed me that the flight had been delayed until 1715 hours. Needless to say, I was livid as were many other passengers. But there was nothing I could do but resign myself to my plight.

I walked away with a heavy heart. As I went by the beverage dispenser, I got a cold drink. There were plenty of empty seats, so I chose one with a clear view out of the window. I reached into my carry-on bag to get my book. I hadn't picked it up since I'd put it in my carry-on just before landing. I tried to read, but I couldn't concentrate. I just sat there watching other people.

On the stroke of 1700 hours, an airline agent appeared at the exit door. Passengers began rushing toward the door. Through the window, I could see that there were buses lined up to take us to the plane. Passengers were taking no chances about getting a seat on the bus. They pushed and shoved one another mercilessly as they rushed out the door. Since there was no systematic order for boarding the buses, the agent had no way to check boarding passes. As a matter of fact, she had stepped aside to keep from being trampled. It was apparent that she was left helpless, and the boarding process was completely out of control.

Just as I got to the door to go out to board a bus, the agent stopped me. In a very abrupt tone of voice, she told me, "You can't board the bus, because there are no more seats on the plane."

I became indignant and showed her my boarding pass. While she looked at it, I demanded, "What do you mean there are no more seats on the plane? My reservation to board this flight was made weeks ago, and it was confirmed just yesterday at the ticket office downtown, and I always reserve a window seat when I make my reservations. My seat number is 15K, as you can plainly see."

With that, she told me, "I will call the pilot."

She picked up the wall phone. I stood right there as she made the call. When she hung up, with no feedback to me as to what the pilot had told her, she curtly said, "Follow me."

I followed her. She led me to a waiting bus. I got on. There were no other passengers on the bus, but the driver took me to the plane. I got off of the bus and walked up the steps and onto the plane.

I walked down the aisle, checking the numbers. When I got to row 15, a man was sitting in window seat number 15K. He was reading. I excused myself to the passengers in the aisle seat and middle seat and leaned over them. I held up my boarding pass stub and said to the gentleman in 15K, "Excuse me, sir, but you're in my seat."

He looked up at me. He didn't say a word. I made a snap judgment that he didn't speak English.

I was still holding up my boarding pass stub. He understood enough English to know that whatever I said had something to do with the seat number and where he was sitting. He reached into his shirt pocket and very confidently showed me his boarding pass stub with seat number 15K printed on it.

With no delay, I rushed to the first flight attendant I saw, showed her my boarding pass stub, and pleaded my case. After checking with the gentleman sitting in 15K, she confirmed that the two of us had been assigned to the same seat number in error.

She said nothing but led me to the center aisle of the cabin where there were two empty seats right behind the bulkhead. She pointed to the seat on the aisle and said, "Sit right there."

I sat down. She walked away. I heaved a sigh of relief, and began to cool off. To be honest, at that point I didn't care where I sat, just so I had a seat on that plane to New York and then back to San Francisco, California, USA.

In a few minutes, the plane took off. The captain's voice came over the public address system with the announcement, "Welcome to Air Afrique for your flight to JFK Airport in New York. We hope you enjoy your flight, and our crew will do everything possible to make you comfortable." From his accent, I could tell that our pilot was an African.

Immediately, I comforted myself in knowing that we'd make a smooth landing if nothing else went right, judging from all of the previous landings that were discernibly smoother than most.

I settled myself in and watched the updates on the big-screen television monitor. Thankfully, our ascent was smooth, and soon after we reached cruising speed, the attendants began their duties by taking orders for beverages.

As I looked around, just as it had been each time before, the passengers were a mix of races, colors, sizes, and nationalities. And there was a mix of many languages spoken in conversation back and forth and across the aisles. Nostalgia set in. I was traveling alone this time. My mind went back to the other two times when Birdie and I had traveled to and from Dakar together. For the moment, I wished she had been with me for this whole experience.

It wasn't long before the attendants began serving our meal as we crossed the Atlantic Ocean. Steak, baked potato, and salad must have been the favorite or staple menu for Air Afrique, because that's what we were served again on this flight. While I ate, I kept reflecting on what I would yet encounter when I tried to make a significant unavoidable revision to my flight schedule in order to get home. I couldn't predict the outcome, so not having a clue as to when I'd get out of New York, I decided to let my mind rest and worry about it when that time came.

As soon as my tray was removed, I nestled back in my seat and positioned my pillow so I could take a nap.

I must have slept during most of the remainder of the flight, because I was awakened by an attendant who was passing out those hot wet washcloths. I knew then that in an hour or so, we'd be landing at JFK.

Schedule changes in New York welled up in my mind again. What on earth was I going to do and what was going to happen when I got to New York? But my greatest fear was that I'd have to spend the night in the terminal and get a flight out the next day. I tried to be optimistic, but it wasn't easy. I drew on my perpetual faith again.

As soon as I got to the terminal, I'd phone Gaines and let him know that I'd be late arriving. By that time, we were ordered to prepare for landing. I sat perfectly motionless until then. Reaffirming my confidence in a smooth touchdown, that pilot, like each of the other African pilots, set us down with almost no impact. I couldn't feel it when we landed.

I gathered up my belongings and made my way up the aisle to get off the plane. I was the first passenger off that flight to go through immigration. Before I left the area, I asked the immigration officer, "How do I get to the domestic terminal?"

Motioning in the direction, he said, "Go down to ground transportation and take a red, white, and blue airport shuttle to Terminal 3."

I followed his directions and that put me in front of Delta Airlines. I walked up to the one ticket counter that was still open. There were two agents behind the counter. It appeared to me that they were reviewing end-of-the-day records. I spoke to them. They looked up at me and smiled as their eyes met mine.

I told them that my flight from Dakar had been delayed. Therefore, I needed to reschedule on the earliest flight I could get.

"Where are you going?" they asked.

I felt stupid, because that was the first thing I should've told them. So I humbly presented my ticket.

After close scrutiny, she said, "There are no more flights out tonight to San Francisco. You'll have to wait until tomorrow morning."

My heart sank to ground level, and I couldn't hold back the tears.

Right away, the other agent offered an alternative by saying, "But we can book you on a flight from here to Los Angeles and then from Los Angeles to San Francisco. That flight departs in fifty minutes."

My spirits lifted. "Gladly, I'll take the flight to Los Angeles and then the flight to San Francisco. May I have a window seat on both flights?" I asked.

"Yes," she answered as she finished her processing.

She handed boarding passes to me. I stood there at the counter a moment while I checked flight numbers. She then directed me to my departing gate.

With a prayer, I again admitted that God had His arms around me and would see me back home safely, even though I was delayed. I couldn't help myself as tears of joy and thankfulness streamed down my face. I thanked the ticket agent profusely as I left the counter.

Lightheartedly, I took off.

On my way to the gate, I stopped at a phone booth and called Gaines to tell him of my arrival time. He said, "OK, beautiful. (That's what he called me.) I'm sorry for the delay, but I thank God you're safe. I'll be glad to see you whenever you get here."

I took a seat in the gate area to wait for flight call. As I sat there, I relived in my mind bits and pieces of my naming ceremony, my trip to and from the village of Santhiousine, and my talk with Mamadou's spiritual leader. Softly, I practiced saying my new Senegalese name and felt sentimental about its meaning and the way I got it.

In that subdued, solemn ceremony held in the parlor of the home of Mamadou Niang—in Dakar, Senegal, West Africa—I, Jane Elizabeth Banks McIntosh, an African-American, was given my Senegal African name: Fatou Ndoye—"Fatou" meaning "caring sister" and "Ndoye" meaning "completeness."

In spite of my terrifying flight across the Atlantic and some frustrating scenarios, my purpose was accomplished, and my heart was filled with pride. No occurrence or episode could diminish or detract from the empirical knowledge I had gained. I will cherish the experiences forever.

I thanked God for His many, many blessings.

The flights from New York to Los Angeles and then on to San Francisco are a blur to me now. But at my journey's end, I felt wholly fulfilled. I couldn't wait to share my precious memories with my dear husband, Gaines, when I finally got home to him in Hayward.

He was fascinated as I recounted the highlights to him and told him that my first name, Fatou, was after Mamadou's sister's name and my last name, Ndoye, was Madame Gueye's maiden name. He smiled as I told him that they both wanted me to bear their names, because that would forever endear me to them and them to me as sisters.

For his sake, I soft-pedaled the downside.

As it had been before his doctors insisted that I take a break, Gaines was in and out of the hospital the next three weeks.

On March 10, 2001, I had to give him up forever to his God.

As I mourned his loss, there was a stream of house calls and telephone calls of condolence and expressions of love for the both of us from family and friends.

One day when I was reminiscing about my naming ceremony event, I went to my study and composed a letter to Air Afrique. In it, I poured out on paper all of the venom stored away in my heart. After the postal clerk processed my letter, I turned from the counter and left the post office. It's difficult to describe my emotions during those moments. All I can say is that I felt purged, and yet, fulfilled.

Gradually, over the next few weeks, I collected my thoughts, and I began to reintegrate into a daily routine with purpose and to project for my future as a widow, including my resolve to write about my extraordinary, once-in-a-lifetime experiences.

In spite of all that had happened for me and to me in such a short span of time, I thanked my God again and asked Him to bless me with the privilege of some day returning to my Motherland.

NAMING CEREMONY CERTIFICATE

for

JANE   ELIZABETH   BANKS   McINTOSH

Born in Colfax, Iowa, U.S.A.

Given her Senegalese Name

In her Naming Ceremony

Held on

Monday, the nineteenth day of February in the year of two thousand one

First name: *FATOU*   Last name: *NDOYE*

Fatou (Caring Sister)   **Ndoye (Completeness)**

In the Parlor at the Home of

MAMADOU NIANG

Dakar, Senegal

West Africa

Signed _____

978-0-595-42257-9
0-595-42257-8